William Stanley Jevons and the Cutting Edge of Economics

William Stanley Jevons was one of the founding fathers of modern economic thought, whose work marked a new chapter in its history, bridging the gap between classical and neo-classical economics. In this ambitious and incisive work, Bert Mosselmans provides a synthetic approach to Jevons' theory and policy.

Adopting a relativist approach to his subject, Mosselmans focuses on many aspects of Jevons' theory, aiming to tie the different strands together where appropriate, but to discriminate where necessary. Thoroughly comprehensive throughout, Mosselmans situates Jevons within the history of economic thought and in relation to his logic, ethics, religion and aesthetics. This reflexive position allows Mosselmans to examine the relation between Jevons' theory and his practice.

The history of economic thought is taught throughout Europe, North America and Japan, and this work would appeal to economists, academics and postgraduates interested in this field. Mosselmans' historiographical approach to Jevons may also be of considerable interest to scholars in philosophy, history and even literature.

Bert Mosselmans is an associate professor in Economics and Philosophy at Roosevelt Academy.

Routledge Studies in the History of Economics

William Stanley Jevons and the Cutting Edge of Economics

Bert Mosselmans

Routledge
Taylor & Francis Group

LONDON AND NEW YORK

First published 2007
by Routledge

Published 2014 by Routledge
2 Park Square, Milton Park, Abingdon, Oxfordshire OX14 4RN

Simultaneously published in the USA and Canada
by Routledge
711 Third Avenue, New York, NY 10017

First issued in paperback 2014

Routledge is an imprint of the Taylor & Francis Group, an informa business

British Library Cataloguing in Publication Data
A catalogue record for this book is available from the British Library

Library of Congress Cataloging-in-Publication Data
Mosselmans, Bert
  Jevons' economics: William Stanley Jevons and the cutting edge of
  economics/Bert Mosselmans
  p.cm.
  Includes biographical references and index
  ISBN-13: 978-0-415-28578-0
  1. Jevons, William Stanley, 1835–1882. 2. Economists–Great Britain–
  Biography. 3. Economics–Great Britain–History–19th century. I. Title
  HB103.J5M67 2007
  330.15'7092–dc22
                      2006025204

ISBN 978-0-415-28578-0 (hbk)
ISBN 978-0-415-86306-3 (pbk)

Aan mijn vader

Jan Baptiste Mosselmans (1941–2006)

Contents

Preface

This book grew out of my doctoral dissertation *From Classical to Neoclassical: the Economic Thought of William Stanley Jevons (1835–1882) and its Relation to his Ethics, Logic and Aesthetics* (1999), which received the Joseph Dorfman Award of the History of Economics Society in 2001. The book is a collection of previously published articles. As many of these articles were published in books or non-economic journals, it seemed a good idea to group them into one single publication. All chapters can be read separately but, at the same time, I have tried to arrange and slightly revise the papers to build up an interdisciplinary exploration of Jevons' thought.

First, we provide an overview of Jevons' biography and economic works (Chapter 1). Thereafter, we investigate Jevons' own perception of the 'marginal revolution' by attempting to reconstruct his views on the Canon in the history of economic thought (Chapter 2). The remaining chapters extend the image of Jevons beyond economics. We start by investigating Quetelet's influence on Jevons' use of statistical and empirical methods (Chapter 3), and then we relate these views to Jevons' work in logic and philosophy of science (Chapter 4). A mechanical view of the world appears, but Jevons' works on economic and social policy indicate that there is some room for institutions in his thought (Chapter 5). A broader image of Jevons emerges when we take his general social and cultural background into account, and especially his views on religion and evolutionary theory (Chapter 6). Finally, we apply this broader image by investigating Jevons' views on music and their consequences for social policy (Chapter 7).

Middelburg, 8 August 2005

1 Jevons and economics

Biography and overview[1]

(with Michael V. White, Monash University, Australia)

Introduction

William Stanley Jevons was one of the great Victorian polymaths, his published work encompassing political economy (economics), logic, statistics and the epistemology and methodology of science. Jevons' training and work in aspects of physics, and especially chemistry and meteorology, was used in generating new concepts and frameworks of analysis, two aspects of which can be noted here. The first was in the *Theory of Political Economy*, where Jevons presented a new approach to value and distribution using metaphors from mechanics. That text, in conjunction with the work of Léon Walras, laid the analytical groundwork for what was subsequently termed microeconomics. The second aspect was in his analyses of commercial fluctuations (today: business cycles). Here, Jevons used his training in meteorology in both graphing complex groups of economic variables and using statistical techniques to analyse them.

While Jevons' work encompasses texts of a theoretical and applied form, it is also important to note that he wrote for a wider audience than those interested in some of the more technical work referred to above. This includes his collection of essays, *Methods of Social Reform*, in which Jevons discussed questions of political economy in a far broader framework than that considered, for example, in the *Theory of Political Economy*. The general theory that he used in all his work, to both analyse and suggest policies for social phenomena, was a particular version of utilitarianism. The *Methods* uses this approach in considering a number of contemporary policy questions while not restricting it to political economy questions. Perhaps the most detailed explanation of Jevons' utilitarianism as applied to policy questions can be found in *The State in Relation to Labour*, first published in 1882. Here, although specifically concerned with questions regarding labour (working conditions and the distribution of income and wealth), Jevons provided a detailed rationale for his use of utilitarianism both to analyse issues and to prescribe associated policies.

Jevons' attempts to discuss issues of political economy for a wider audience can also be seen in two other texts. The first is in his *Political Economy* (1878), a rather rare text today, which was composed for teachers and pupils in secondary schools. This little book was also important because it explained a number of concepts that he used but did not explain in his *Theory of Political Economy*. The second is his *Principles of Economics*, which was incomplete at the time of Jevons' death. Because of difficulties with assembling the text and problems associated with the first editor, this text was not published until 1905, edited by Henry Higgs. There has sometimes been a tendency to characterize the *Principles* as unimportant because of its incomplete form. It does, however, contain some valuable information regarding Jevons' initial work in political economy from the 1860s and his later work. The volume is also important because it reprints a number of pamphlets and talks by Jevons, which both amplify his theoretical approach and provide a clear illustration of how he thought that approach should be applied to policy questions.

Jevons' life[2]

William Stanley Jevons was born in Liverpool on 1 September 1835. His family was Unitarian and part of a large group of intellectual and progressive families knotted together by intermarriage. His father Thomas Jevons (1791–1855) was an iron merchant who combined the practical sense of a man of business with much intellectual curiosity and a flair for invention. His mother, Mary Anne Roscoe (1795–1845), grew up in an intellectual and artistic milieu and showed much interest in poetry, chemistry, logic, botany and political economy. She died in 1845, when Jevons was ten years old. His older sister, Lucy Jevons (1830–1910), became a substitute mother, supporting Jevons morally and encouraging him in his intellectual development. He was, however, much closer to his younger sister Henrietta (1839–1909): they both loved music, exchanged their ideas about religion and shared their emotions. Henrietta (Henny) lost her mental balance in 1869, a few months after the death of Jevons' oldest brother Roscoe Jevons (1829–1869). Roscoe was interested in poetry, chemistry and mathematics and should be seen as a major intellectual influence on young William Stanley. Unfortunately, he became insane shortly after his mother's death. Another brother was Herbert Jevons (1831–1874). Herbert had bad health, was unable to settle to a career for many years and finally became employed in New Zealand, where he died at the early age of forty-two. Jevons' youngest brother Thomas or Tommy (1841–1917) is portrayed as a very intelligent but somewhat lazy young student. He migrated to America and became a successful businessman.

The early death of his mother and the mental and physical illnesses of his brothers and sisters left their mark on the development of the young Jevons. The so-called railway boom crisis of 1847 should also be seen as an important event in his life, as it caused the bankruptcy of his father's firm. The railway crisis resulted from the pressure of increasingly vast accumulations of capital for investment; the capital glut encouraged bad investments and, therefore, the production of capital-absorbing railways was growing at a high rate. When profits remained absent, railway production was checked, and the demand for iron, which had grown during the 'railway boom', fell dramatically. The Jevonses were some of the unfortunate iron merchants driven into bankruptcy.

William Stanley Jevons went to University College School in London in 1850, at the age of fifteen, and in 1851, he became a student at the University College. He remained there until 1852, but did not finish his education. Instead, he accepted a position as an assayer at the Australian Mint (see below). He studied chemistry under Graham and Williamson, two pioneers in the development of atomic theory and the theory of molecular motion. Chemistry remained important during Jevons' life, and he even published two papers on Brownian Motion in 1870 and 1878. Another major influence at University College was Augustus De Morgan (1806–1871), with his courses on mathematics and logic. Jevons' own approaches to scientific method, probability, logic and mathematics were influenced by De Morgan. Jevons also had a lively interest in botany, which probably stemmed from his mother. Jevons' interest in political economy is not surprising, given his non-conformist intellectual and family background, but it can also be explained by the context of economic development in which he lived, with both its dark and its good sides. We have already mentioned Jevons' 'hereditary reasons' for not overlooking business fluctuations, as many members of his family had been bankrupted. But London's situation in the early 1850s already encouraged an interest in social and economic life. Outbreaks of cholera and bad sanitary conditions came to light as major social problems. Könekamp writes about the 'sanitary age' and states that Dickens' propaganda for sanitary and social reform influenced Jevons, who was brought up in Unitarian circles concerned with social improvement. Jevons undertook long walks through the poor and manufacturing parts of London. But the 1850s were years of rising British economic power as well, reflected in the Great Exhibition of the Works of All Nations, held in 1851. This exhibition quickened the pride of everyone, and Jevons visited it several times. It probably aroused Jevons' interest in 'the industrial mechanism of society', which also dates from 1851 (see Jevons' remark in Jevons 1905: vii). All those contextual elements help to explain why much of Jevons' economic work is concerned with business cycles, economic growth and decline, and improvement of social conditions and education.

Jevons left University College without taking his degree. He planned to go into business in Liverpool at the end of the 1853 session. In his diary entry for 16 January 1853, he elaborates on his willingness to pursue a business career and to continue his education in his spare time (Black and Könekamp 1972: 77–80). His dream was to collect financial means in his business career, and then to retire and to devote the rest of his life to scientific enquiries. His father regarded these aspirations as somewhat illusory. In this context, the lucrative job offer as an assayer came up. Jevons was not at all keen to leave for Australia, but the interesting salary of an assayer would lighten the financial burdens of his family.

Jevons sailed from Liverpool on 29 June 1854 and arrived in Melbourne on 6 October. At first, his financial position was rather tight, but this changed in January 1855 when he was offered full-time employment at the Mint. Initially, Jevons found the assaying business exciting: he experimented and even wrote an article on 'Gold Assay', which appeared in Watt's *Dictionary of Chemistry* (1864). However, after April 1855, it became a sinecure, and he devoted much more time to other scientific investigations. Jevons' 'science of man' project entailed an interdisciplinary utilitarian approach to different aspects of individual and social life. His work covered many different areas, as is shown by the bibliography collected by Inoue and White (1993): railway policy, meteorology, protection, land policy, cloud formation, gunpowder and lightning, geology, etc. Jevons established a detailed meteorological account of Australia and studied the city of Sydney and, not surprisingly, the problem of sanitation received a central place in these investigations. Another study in this context is Jevons' work on 'division of labour' and 'classification of occupations': Jevons wanted to investigate how the interaction of different kinds of labour resulted in 'the industrial mechanism of society'. Much has been written about Jevons' early influences in Australia. An important road to Jevons' political economy may be the 'railway discussion' to which he devoted three articles. According to Jevons, the extension of railways is acceptable only if the gains are in accordance with the outlays, and this should be measured by people's willingness to pay higher fares. It is clear that this applies to the case of direct benefits, but Jevons states that the same must hold true for so-called indirect benefits. If people are not willing to pay higher fares, then it proves that they do not see possible indirect effects in the future that would justify higher expenses in the present. Insolvent railways would mean 'unproductive expenditure' and a public debt, and this would limit the productive powers of the country.[3] Jevons' 'science of man' project not only included his surveys on the mechanism of society, the division of labour and social and moral improvement through the establishment of sanitation, but also an investigation of the role of art and especially of music in a person's life (see Chapter 7).

Jevons left Australia in 1859 and returned to University College in London to complete his education. The justification for his departure home is couched in economic terms regarding 'preparation' and 'performance' or even (human) 'capital' and 'labour'. It is better to spend some years in acquiring skills than to start hammering at once, and Jevons would like to continue his education in order to receive a higher social position in the future (Black 1973: 359–60). The early 1860s are important for Jevons' intellectual development, and he reports in his diary that he received significant insights in both economics and logic: a 'true comprehension of value' (La Nauze 1953; Black 1981: 120) and the 'substitution of similars' (Black 1972a: 179, see Chapter 6).

Jevons received his MA degree in 1862 and was awarded the gold medal 'in the third branch', which included logic, moral philosophy, political philosophy, history of philosophy and political economy. He became a member of the Volunteer Movement, a 'home guard' formed to oppose the French armies of Napoleon III in case of an invasion. Jevons wanted to be a publicist and earn his living by writing and publishing articles; he must have had in mind the ease with which he contributed to the Australian press. It proved to be more difficult than Jevons expected: most of his contributions were rejected. All his articles appearing in journals in 1862 were concerned exclusively with meteorology and natural science (see Inoue and White 1993: 128–9). He published two diagrams at his own expense, but they did not receive much attention. The first diagram shows 'all the Weekly Accounts of the Bank of England, since the passing of the Bank Act of 1844', and the second diagram depicts 'the Price of English Funds, the Price of Wheat, the Number of Bankruptcies, and the Rate of Discount, Monthly, since 1731'. Both diagrams were updated and reprinted in *Investigations in Currency and Finance*. Jevons presented two papers at the 1862 meeting of the Economic Science and Statistics Section of the British Association: 'On the Study of Periodic Commercial Fluctuations' and his famous paper 'Notice of a General Mathematical Theory of Political Economy'. This latter paper can be seen as a summary of his later work, *The Theory of Political Economy*, first published nine years later. Neither paper received much attention, and Jevons was very disappointed by this lack of interest (see Black 1962).

In 1863, Jevons was appointed as a tutor at Owens College, Manchester, and finally his financial worries came to an end. It must have been a rather difficult job, as it included giving tuition to backward students, and the general standard of the students was rather low. At first, Jevons did not like Manchester's smoky environment at all, but he could appreciate the city's 'distinguished literary position'.[4] Jevons visited many libraries, started an impressive collection of private books and undertook much bibliographical work.[5] 1863 was not only the year of his appointment to Owens College, it was also the starting point of his successful publication career. In 1863, *A Serious Fall in the Value of Gold* was published (reprinted in *Investigations in Currency and Finance*) and, for the first time, Jevons became recognized as a political economist. In 1865, *The Coal Question* appeared, a work that was quoted by John Stuart Mill in the House of Commons. Jevons was appointed lecturer in political economy and logic for the 1865–6 session at Owens College, and could therefore resign his tutorship.[6] He disliked teaching in Manchester, but it served as a means of overcoming his fear of speaking in public. The evening classes were especially hard, and they took place in unhealthy conditions. Moreover, Jevons seriously damaged his health because he would not let his teaching interfere with his research. Black (1993: 175–6) argues that precisely Jevons' attitude towards research should be seen as an improvement regarding the institutionalization of economics at British universities. Like his cousin, H. E. Roscoe, Jevons pursued the 'new academic policy of research', which resulted in the conception of a university as something more than simply a teaching institution.[7] Jevons' research resulted in two important works in the history of science: *The Theory of Political Economy* (1871) and *The Principles of Science* (1874).

In 1867, Jevons married Harriet A. Taylor, and they subsequently had one son and two daughters. He and his family moved to London in 1876, on his taking up a chair at University College. The fact that Jevons accepted a loss of income as a result of this move indicates that he did not take the new job in London out of professional ambition. On the contrary, for health reasons, Jevons wanted less responsibility (Black 1993: 180). Moreover, he had always wanted to live the life of a 'literary man', and this was only possible through a reduction in his teaching responsibilities. London was also a literary centre, and Jevons liked having libraries and publishers within reach. In 1878, Jevons published two works written for a larger audience: *Money and the Mechanism of Exchange* and *Political Economy*. In the last period of his short life, Jevons focused on his well-known sunspot theory (several articles are published in *Investigations in Currency and Finance*) and on social reform (e.g. *The State in Relation to Labour*, 1882). Rosamond Könekamp describes the circumstances of his death:

> Jevons' life was ended by a tragic accident; he was drowned near Hastings on 13th August, 1882, when nearly 47. [. . .] He was drowned on almost the last day of his stay at the seaside with his family. He had loved swimming since childhood, but his health was not good at this time and he knew he should not bathe. [. . .] However, as the last day drew near he could no longer resist, and he did go for a bathe without telling his wife. No one saw what happened, but the sea was quite rough at the time, and his strength cannot have been equal to it.
>
> (Könekamp 1962: 272–3)

Methods of Social Reform (1883) and *Investigations in Currency in Finance* (1884) are posthumously published collections of earlier essays. In 1905, Jevons' unfinished manuscript *The Principles of Economics* appeared.

The Theory of Political Economy

Although Jevons published a good deal of work on applied economics (see below), he is still best known to economists for his *Theory of Political Economy* (*TPE*, 1871, 1879a). This sets out his basic theoretical explanation for the relative prices of commodities (involving the question of 'value') and the distribution of output as income. While the analysis showed some degree of theoretical continuity with the work of his predecessors, such as John Stuart Mill, it rested on four components that together constituted an analytical break with preceding discussions of value and distribution. The four components were characteristic of what subsequently became known as 'neo-classical' or 'marginalist' economics.

The first was to represent economic behaviour as a type of mechanics. In formulating the theory as 'the mechanics of utility and self-interest' (Jevons 1879a: XX), Jevons drew on his training and work in particular aspects of the natural sciences. The nub of *TPE* was formulated between 1860 and 1862, when Jevons made behaviour analogous to 'forces' in physics, such as those of gravity. By 1871, he regarded his approach as broadly consistent with the new physics of 'energy', which had been developed since the 1850s (Mirowski 1989; Schabas 1990).

The second component was the extensive use of mathematics which, for Jevons, meant the calculus and the mid-Victorian representation of Euclidean geometry. The mathematics were necessary for the third component, which was the representation of behaviour and market activity in functional forms. The functional approach was consistent with the underlying stimulus–response 'model' of behaviour. Adapting the utilitarian theory of Jeremy Bentham, Jevons argued that all behaviour was driven by the pursuit of pleasure (utility) and the avoidance of pain (disutility). Given the assumption of wealth maximization, economic activity was depicted in terms of equilibrium positions in which there was a 'balance' of marginal utility and disutility. While the motive 'forces' referred to individual behaviour, individuals *per se* played no part in the analysis, as the theory depicted 'representative' or 'average' economic actors who did not actually exist. However, Jevons claimed that, statistically, an average of aggregate behaviour – the 'fictitious mean' – would mirror the behaviour depicted in the theoretical model (see Chapter 3). It should be noted that, while *TPE* assumed that actors were driven solely by the maximization of wealth, Jevons made clear that wealth was only one aspect to be taken into account when assessing the results of economic policies and the overall social utility of human actions (see Chapter 5).

The fourth component of the analysis was to recast the theoretical problem posed in a value and distribution analysis. For Jevons, the 'problem of economics' was to maximize the utility of the output obtained from a set of given resources:

> Given, a certain population, with various needs and powers and production, in possession of certain lands and other sources of material: required, the mode of employing their labour which will maximise the utility of the produce.
>
> (Jevons 1879a: 267)

In depicting economic activity as a form of constrained maximization, Jevons illustrated the importance of the physics metaphors that underpinned *TPE*. At the same time, the statement above announced a substantial departure from the work of his predecessors for whom variations in population, explained by some form of the Malthusian 'population principle', were an integral component of a theory of value and distribution. It should be noted that, while the population principle was reduced to a parameter in Jevons' core analysis, he used the principle elsewhere, as in *The Coal Question* when explaining a series of possible long-period changes in the economy.

Jevons presented the analysis of *TPE* in seven chapters. After an Introduction, which defended the use of mathematics and alluded to some of the difficulties in statistically 'verifying' the analysis, Chapters II and III set out the utilitarian theory of behaviour and its application in the form of the marginal utility theory to explain the consumption (or purchasing) of commodities. Chapter IV used that theory to discuss trading or exchange in a market period, in which the supply of commodities was given. In the basic model, exchange took place between 'trading bodies' in wholesale markets such as for raw cotton and wheat. In general, such markets were deemed to be 'perfectly' competitive in that all commodities were homogeneous and there were no restraints on trading with large numbers of transactors. At any moment, brokers set a uniform price, which Jevons called 'the law of indifference', although the price would change with each set of trades. The equilibrium condition then entailed that the ratio of exchange for two commodities would equal the reciprocal of the ratio of the marginal utilities of the commodities

(Jevons 1879a: 95). The marginal utility ratio would in turn equal the commodity price ratio. The formulation of the equilibrium condition was a striking example of Jevons' use of mechanical metaphors. As he explained in the second edition, it was based on that for a lever (or 'balance') in static equilibrium.

The remainder of *TPE* was principally concerned with long-period positions towards which the economy would tend in a series of market periods. Chapter V dealt with changes in production levels (and hence changes in supply conditions for different market periods), describing a long-period position when the ratio of the cost of production of commodities was equal to their marginal utility and price ratios. This analysis of cost of production, which appeared in the second edition, now appears odd, for the only costs considered were those of labour, although the workforce was clearly working with raw materials.

The last three chapters outlined Jevons' distribution analysis. Chapter VI explained that rent, the return to owners of land used to produce raw materials, was not part of the cost of production as it was price determined. It depended on the relative fertility of the land, with the last unit employed paying no rent. This was, as Jevons acknowledged, a result very similar to that of his predecessors. Chapter VII then provided an explanation of the rate of interest on capital in a highly original, if flawed, analysis. Interest was the return for abstaining from consumption in providing capital that increased productivity by lengthening production periods. 'Free' capital was defined as a sum of money or a bundle of commodities used to maintain the workforce for constructing an investment project. The amount of capital invested would, however, depend on both the quantity of capital and the time for which it was invested. The rate of interest, which would tend to equality across the economy as a result of competition, depended on the rate of increase in output compared with the amount of capital invested. Because output would increase at a decreasing rate, the interest rate would tend to fall. Jevons regarded this as a statistical 'fact'. The analysis assumed a given workforce whose share of the output produced was depicted as a residual, depending on the amount of capital invested.

Jevons drew on that explanation in the last chapter when he summarized the distribution analysis. In a long-period position with given prices and rent put to one side as price determined, the distribution of the remaining output was explained in a sequence with the interest rate determined first. Investment in new industries or products would initially produce above-average returns, but these would be reduced under the pressure of competition from new investments, reducing the interest rate to a competitive minimum. While wage rates would initially depend on the state of competition in an industry, in the long run, wages would depend on the demand and supply for different types of labour. This meant, according to Jevons, that 'the competition to obtain proper workmen will strongly tend to secure to the latter all their legitimate share in the ultimate produce [. . .] Every labourer ultimately receives the due value of his produce after paying a proper fraction to the capitalist' (Jevons 1879a: XX). Jevons was dissatisfied with that analysis and, in the Preface to the second edition, he announced a new approach, in which rent would form part of the cost of production and wages would be explained in analogous terms. A detailed explanation of this approach would have necessitated recasting much of the text, but that task was never undertaken. It may have been described in the *Principles of Economics*, but that text was largely unfinished when Jevons drowned. Some hints regarding the wages analysis can, however, be found in *The State in Relation to Labour* (1882).

The second edition of *TPE* was important not only for signalling a new approach to distribution but also because Jevons considerably expanded the text, explaining concepts and arguments that were only hinted at or referred to briefly in the first edition. Of particular importance, as was noted above, is his explanation of how his basic equation of exchange was taken from that for a lever in static equilibrium in mechanics. Other passages were added dealing with, for example, cost of production and a long-period equilibrium position for the economy (Chapter V). In the fourth edition, his son, Herbert Stanley Jevons, added a number of editorial comments to the text and three new appendices. One appendix consisted of a series of notes on capital that Jevons had intended for publication in the *Principles of Economics*. These notes, which had apparently been overlooked, serve to reinforce the point that *TPE* was by no means a complete statement of Jevons' approach to value and distribution.

Monetary economics and business cycles: methodological achievements

Jevons' contribution to empirical economics is substantial (see Stigler 1982; Aldrich 1987; Morgan 1990). *A Serious Fall in the Value of Gold* (1863, reprinted in *Investigations in Currency and Finance*) computes index numbers using a geometric mean, which was a remarkable and novel methodology for Jevons' time. These calculations were then used to investigate the influence of the Australian and Canadian gold discoveries of 1851 on the general price level. Jevons justified the use of the geometric mean by arguing that multiplicative disturbances would be balanced against each other. As there was no empirical verification of this hypothesis, Stigler argued that the absence of a probabilistic analysis should be seen as an anomaly in Jevons' work. His *Principles of Science* (1874), however, contains an elaborate discussion of probability: it enters when complete knowledge is absent, as a measure of ignorance.[8] Aldrich argues that Jevons used probability in two main patterns of argument. The first approach entails the application of the 'inverse method' in induction: if many observations suggest regularity, then it becomes highly improbable that these result from mere coincidence. In *A Serious Fall*, a large majority of commodities show a rise in price and thus a rise in exchange value relative to gold. Here, Jevons argued that a depreciation of gold is much more probable than mere coincidences leading to the rise in prices. The second approach was the method of least squares, which Jevons used when he gave more weight to commodities that were less vulnerable to price fluctuations. He thus tried to fit empirical laws starting from a priori reasoning about the form of the equation. Although these approaches show that Jevons had at least some concern for probability and the theory of errors, his analysis remains incomplete when judged by present standards. We should, however, keep in mind that Jevons was a pioneer in econometrics and that he worked within the limits of his mathematical understanding. *A Serious Fall* is remembered not so much for its limited use of probability theory, but rather for its construction of index numbers.

Jevons' monetary economics

Jevons' work on money and monetary economics can be found in many surveys and articles, most of them reprinted posthumously in *Investigations in Currency and Finance* (1884). A popular treatment of the subject also appeared in his *Money and the Mechanism of Exchange* (1875). Laidler (1982) argues that Jevons' ideas are in accordance with the monetary orthodoxy of his time, and that he should be considered conservative for defending the 1844 Bank Charter Act. This Act established a system of gold coin with convertible paper. Whereas the issue of convertible paper was regulated by the government in accordance with the bullion holdings of the Bank of England, most other banking matters remained unregulated. For Jevons, monetary institutions should be aware of seasonal fluctuations and business cycles and alter the amount of money in circulation accordingly to meet public demand. All other forms of intervention should be avoided. Jevons favoured the gold standard over the silver standard: silver coins would be needlessly heavy. The natural course for prosperous nations was to adopt a single gold standard, and the gold supplies seemed to be sufficient to fulfil this role, whereas silver supplies were so abundant that they should be used for other purposes. Jevons argued that a double standard (of gold and silver) would be less exposed to fluctuations than a single standard, but preferred the gold standard for reasons of simplicity. Moreover, a bimetallic standard would revert to a silver standard because of the relative depreciation of the latter metal (Jevons 1884: 278–303).

Business cycles and sunspots

Jevons first began serious work on the analysis of 'commercial fluctuations' (now termed business cycles) in a large unpublished work of the early 1860s, which he called the 'Statistical Atlas'. Two principal results from this project appeared in 1862. The first was two large statistical diagrams (subsequently reprinted in *Investigations*), one of which dealt with the long-term effects of changes in the price of wheat on economic activity. The second was a paper entitled 'On the Study of Periodic Fluctuations', presented to the British Association for the Advancement of Science, dealing with a similar topic, albeit on a quarterly and annual basis. This showed average variations from month to month in the rate of discount, the total number of bankruptcies, the average price of consols and the average price of wheat over the last fifteen years. Jevons' study of business cycles was influenced by meteorology, another field in which he made significant contributions. This influence can be seen in two ways. First, Jevons believed that commercial fluctuations were comparable to meteorological fluctuations, and suggested that similar methods and empirical techniques could be used in both cases. Second, Jevons looked for meteorological explanations of business cycles (the sunspot theory, see below). His work on business cycles is also connected with his work on monetary economics, as fluctuations in the money market receive an important place in his analysis. Jevons used averages to eliminate the influence of seasonal fluctuations. He argued that there was an excess of payments in summer, due to agriculture, building, outdoor trades and travelling: more wages were paid and money was used for buying harvest produce. Many labourers did not use banks, and would hold (in the aggregate) considerable amounts of cash, especially of metallic money (which shows a greater variation than bank notes). At first, this drain is met by the reserves of private firms and smaller banks, and these are replenished by the dividends that are paid in October. Normally, the dividends are placed on deposit but, in October, they are generally withdrawn. The Bank of England is therefore acting as a bank of last resort in this month. The note circulation decreases rapidly in November and December. Jevons argues that the system of restricted issuing is perfectly able to meet the problems caused by the annual cycle.

The next step in the development of Jevons' theory of the business cycle was taken when he looked for outward, meteorological explanations of the cycle. In 'The Solar Period and the Price of Corn' (1875), he investigated whether a statistical relationship could be established between the sunspot period and the prices of agricultural products. He first used English agricultural prices between 1259 and 1400, which were supposed to be almost completely determined by local (and thus weather) circumstances. Although dissatisfied with the results, Jevons thought the survey revealed an influence of sunspots on the harvest. Moreover, Jevons argued that economic fluctuations were 'mental' in nature. Mood fluctuations should be explained by outward causes, and he suspected that the sunspots might be influential in that respect. In 'The Periodicity of Commercial Crises and its Physical Explanations' (1878), he tried to prove that a decennial periodicity existed in the activity of trade between 1700 and 1870. The mental state of merchants and bankers was influenced by the success of the harvest, with a connection between the credit cycle and solar activity. Unfortunately, it was impossible to detect a similar variation in the price of corn, because the climatic conditions were much too complicated and the success of the harvest depends on multiple causes. However, Jevons argued that, outside Europe, for instance in India, a clear decennial tendency was visible in periods of abundance and scarcity (Jevons 1884: 187–200). 'Commercial Crises and the Sun-Spots' (1878) mainly has the same content as the previous paper, but relies upon more evidence and the conclusions are extended. Jevons now argues that the recurrence of crises depends mainly on commerce with the East, and especially with India and China, where famines occur with the same periodicity as sunspots. The failure of harvests in the East leads to a reduced exportation of European goods. There is no relationship between the extent of manias or crises and the variation in foreign trade, but this variation forms the impulse for commercial changes in the West. 'The impulse from abroad is like the match which fires the inflammable spirits of the speculative classes' (Jevons 1884: 221).

Much has been written about the absurdity of Jevons' sunspot explanation for business cycles.[9] However, Peart (1991) emphasizes that this theory is much more than a simple meteorological explanation of economic phenomena, because of Jevons' attention to mood fluctuations. Price fluctuations due to harvest failures give rise to changed 'moods' of economic agents. This results in altered investment decisions that multiply the effect of the harvest cycle, especially when 'mistaken' decisions are involved. In any case, Jevons' sunspot theory was not taken seriously by most of his contemporaries. The arguments were far-fetched and his 'inverse method in induction' – the numerical correspondence between business cycle and sunspots is too close to suggest a mere coincidence – did not convince his opponents. The assumption of a period cycle caused from outside the economy was unattractive to most economists, and the empirical methodology was new and unusual in the 1860s and 1870s. Nevertheless, Jevons was one of the first economists to build theories utilizing statistical regularities and relationships in the data. It was not until the 1930s that similar macroeconomic models were formulated in economics.

Social reform

In 1882, Jevons published *The State in Relation to Labour*, in which he elaborates on labour relations and legislation. In 1883, a posthumous collection of earlier essays on social reform and policy was published, entitled *Methods of Social Reform*. Both works were influenced by utilitarianism and Unitarianism. Utilitarianism appears when Jevons tries to evaluate policy measures according to the principle of 'the greatest good of the greatest number'. Unitarianism is visible in Jevons' vision of the goal of social policy and legislation: amelioration of working-class conditions through morally elevating policy measures that give rise to an improvement of working-class 'character' (see White 1994a). For example, Jevons (1879b: 533) discusses the choice between building a free library and establishing a new racecourse. Jevons claims that an analysis of the effects of these measures using Bentham's categories (intensity, length, certainty, . . .) shows that a free library delivers more pleasure than a racecourse. Peart (1990a) remarks that this analysis is unclear and that Jevons' application of utilitarianism contains implicit value judgements 'concerning the general development of society and the amelioration of working class conditions'. This humanitarian orientation was quite common in intellectual middle-class circles in Victorian England, and especially among Unitarians (to which movement Jevons belonged). *Methods of Social Reform* contains several studies that justify policy measures directed to intellectual and moral improvement: establishment of libraries, suppression of the drink traffic in order to diminish drunkenness, establishment of museums (with all items put in a logical order). Jevons pleads for 'experimental legislation': society is too complex for large reforms based upon an elaborate theoretical framework and, therefore, each problem should be studied separately. Legislators should listen to specialists from different relevant fields and to the general public and, for each proposed policy measure, costs and benefits should be balanced against each other. The result is a quest for incremental social reform based on practical wisdom and not on general abstract principles.

Jevons' writings on labour relations fit into this framework. Jevons is not opposed to trade unions as such, but he argues that their actions should be directed to the general good and not to the interests of a specific class or trade. For instance, by establishing entry barriers, trade unions artificially limit the supply of a certain skill, and may therefore extract an additional scarcity rent that would disappear in the case of an entirely free market. Such a situation, in which one trade would receive a larger share than is justified by economic theory, would therefore lead to an inefficient resource allocation. In this sense, monopolistic trade unions are injurious to the consumers, and therefore to working-class people as well. High wages for hat-makers imply high prices for hats, payable by hat-wearers who are mostly members of the working class. A rise in wages for the plasterers would result in less demand for houses, which would lower the wages of bricklayers or carpenters. Workmen belong to the same class, but 'they are and must be competitors'. Moreover, preventing the surplus labour in one trade from entering another results in a decrease in producing power. Jevons concludes that a general increase in wages is impossible, and that monopolistic actions within one trade result in injury to the community in general and to working-class people in particular (Jevons 1882: 106–9).

Jevons votes for heterogeneous co-operative positions instead, as these do not consist of making specific skills artificially scarce. A partnership binding together the interests of employer and workman should be the solution for the labour problem. The employer would advance only a subsistence wage to the labourer, enabling him and his family to survive during the period in between manufacture and sale. After this period, the labourer would receive his share in the surplus profits, or that part 'beyond the necessary charges for interest, wages of superintendence, cost of depreciation of capital, reserve to meet bad debts, and all other expenses of production for which the employer can fairly claim compensation' (Jevons 1882: 143–7). Industrial divisions should be perpendicular, not horizontal: the workman's interests should be bound up with those of his employer's. The workman will then become a shareholder in the firm (Jevons 1882: 149).

In a lecture delivered to the Trade Unionists' Political Association, Jevons identifies three different kinds of objectives of trade unions: (1) acting as insurance societies in favour of the unfortunate workmen; (2) rendering factories more wholesome and safe; and (3) struggling with capitalists in order to raise wages. Only the last activity is illegitimate according to Jevons, as we saw earlier. In the case of insurance activities, trade unions should be organized by combining many grades of workmen and several branches of industry, as this may reduce the amount of selfishness and raise the notion of solidarity instead. Even more important is the second activity, because a single workman is mostly unable to enforce concessions from his employer concerning labour conditions. Workmen should unite in order to force employers to adopt policy measures that improve safety, but also to reduce working hours – especially regarding their children and wives (Jevons 1883: 105–10).[10] In this sense, trade unions may foster wealth, morality and intelligence through an alteration in the attitude and the behaviour of the working class. Jevons refers explicitly to an encouragement of saving, which would lead, in the long run, to a situation in which workmen 'may become in a degree their own capitalists' (Jevons 1883: 120–1). Labourers are, because of the 'character' of the class to which they belong, less inclined to devote much attention to the future. Economic policy should try to change this labour class 'character' and thus encourage saving. Chapters 5–7 explore these issues further.

The Coal Question

The signing in 1860 of the Cobden–Chevalier treaty, which prohibited the use of import duties on coal between Britain and France, was followed by claims that exporting coal to 'the enemy' would undermine British industrial supremacy as coal supplies would be exhausted. In 1863, however, the weapons manufacturer, Sir William Armstrong, argued that the relevant question was not the absolute size of coal reserves, but rather the increasing costs of extracting coal from deeper mines and thinner seams. It was this that would lead to decreasing international competitiveness (White 1991a: 229–30). Jevons used that argument as the basis for his analysis in *The Coal Question* (1865), a book that established his public reputation as an economist after it was cited in Parliament in 1866 by both John Stuart Mill and William Gladstone, the Chancellor of the Exchequer. The book contained an elaborate application of the 'Malthusian' population principle to an industrial economy. With population growth increasing with the prosperity of the country, which was, in turn, dependent on coal, the increasing costs of extraction would mean a loss of international competitiveness compared with low-cost producers such as the United States of America. No other conceivable energy source was available, and technological innovation would, by lowering costs, only increase coal use. As the growth rate fell, capital and skilled labour would emigrate, which meant, Jevons suggested, that Britain would become a nation of handicraft manufacturers. The British Empire, with its culture, science and traditions, would thus be a period of 'brief but true greatness' (Jevons 1865: 454–60).

This analysis was different from much of Jevons' other work in political economy because it was concerned with a series of long periods in a specific historical setting. The timing of the Empire's demise was clearly long term, although Jevons was not particularly clear on the dating. What was evident in the first edition, however, was a rather apocalyptic tone. Subsequently, Jevons expressed less acute pessimism about both the extent of the decline in competitiveness and the effects on the economy. He continued to believe, however, in the general validity of the analysis. Just as Marx waited for the workers' revolution, Jevons waited for the effects of rising coal prices.

Conclusion

Jevons was a great polymath of the nineteenth century, and his contributions to economics, logic and natural science are still regarded as outstanding today. It is therefore surprising to find that Jevons did not establish a real 'school' or followers, in the way in which many economists and scientists did before and after him. One part of the explanation is certainly his early death. It is, however, also possible to find reasons that are related to the peculiar position of Jevons' work within the scientific context of his time. His methodological and statistical proposals were original and novel, and it was therefore difficult to find contemporaries who recognized their significance. The limited availability of relevant statistical material further diminished the perceived usefulness of statistical methods, and the association of Jevons' empirical work with the sunspot theory of business cycles did not increase its respectability. Jevons' theoretical work received several critical reviews, which pointed out that he did not always pay enough attention to all the details and consequences of his arguments. The form of his particular enthusiasm for mathematics and mechanics was not shared by most other economists, and his *Theory of Political Economy* was superseded by the work of Alfred Marshall in his own country and the work of others (notably Walras) elsewhere.

Jevons was, nevertheless, an important model for the professional economist in the twentieth century, with his combined emphasis on theory, practice and policy and his academic attitude of combining teaching with scientific research. His work in such disparate fields as economics, logic and meteorology may have prevented him from working out all the precise details of his projects. On the other hand, he gained a general image of science and methodology from his interdisciplinary research that would be a characteristic of later 'modern' economics. Jevons recognized that economics needs mathematical clarity and that statistics may serve as a means to bridge the gap between economic facts and theory. His intellectual heritage from the natural sciences (especially mechanistic physics and atomistic chemistry) inspired him to develop a mechanical exchange theory that examined static equilibria. His conception of atomistic 'trading bodies' and economic subjects as 'representative agents' was derived from psychology and statistics (see Chapter 3 on Quetelet's influence), which, in conjunction with the calculus, Jevons used to formulate a theory of human behaviour in a functional form, an extraordinary development in the second half of the nineteenth century. The concept of 'utility', derived from the utilitarian tradition in moral philosophy (e.g. Bentham), entered the functional representation of human behaviour and replaced 'labour' as the determinant of value. His practical experience as an assayer at the Australian Mint improved his practical knowledge of economics directly, but it also led him to formulate important metaphors in his *Theory of Political Economy* (e.g. the balance). His work in the field of meteorology inspired him to study business cycles and time series and led to the development of important statistical tools (e.g. index numbers). *The Coal Question* relied heavily upon his knowledge of the physical characteristics of coal and should be seen as one of the first major works in the field of 'energy' economics. In his social writings, Jevons examined the political consequences of his economic theory in a typically utilitarian fashion. It was his interdisciplinary approach that underlay many of his ground-breaking achievements.

2 Jevons and the history of economic thought

Deconstructing the Canon[11]

Introduction

Many textbooks present the history of economic thought as a succession of names and theories. This results in a 'Whig history', a Canon in which an older theory (and author) is replaced by a newer one for 'obvious' rational reasons. Kenneth Boulding argued that this approach may be harmful to a student's perception of the history of economic thought:

> The student first learned what was wrong with Adam Smith and all the things in which he was wrong and confused, then he went on to learn what was the matter with Ricardo, then what was the matter with John Stuart Mill, and then what was the matter with Marshall. Many students never learned anything that was right at all, and I think emerged from the course with the impression that economics was a monumental collection of errors.
>
> (Boulding 1971: 232)

The Canon in the history of economics is not an 'obvious' theoretical framework, it is historical itself. In his 1997 Editorial for the History of Economics Society (HES) mailing list, J. Daniel Hammond discusses the role of 'Taxonomy in History of Economics'. He argues that pressing taxonomies on the history of economic thought may be dangerous. By abstracting and simplifying economic theory, taxonomy allows analysis and understanding. However, 'good taxonomy requires critical attention to both the definition and application of categories and their labels'. Good taxonomy pays attention to biographical circumstances, published writings and the unpublished record of drafts, notes and correspondence.[12] Postmodern historiography argues that history is a language game that contextually develops its own standards of truth. The historian produces his or her own construction out of a virtually unlimited content that is mediated by other historians. As more than one construction is possible, the reader should deconstruct the text and examine for whom it was written. Every 'stream' in history defines itself, which implies that a methodology should be reflexive. Jenkins (1991) argues that we should analyse how texts were written in the past, and that we are in need of methodological reflexive studies about how history is written in the postmodern world. In this chapter, we apply the reflexive notion of historiography to the Canon in the history of economics. We argue that the historical process of de- and reconstruction of a contemporary canon may illuminate the thought of historical authors. They make *their* taxonomy, categories and labels visible in their description of 'the' canon. The study of this process should pay attention to biographical circumstances, the writings and correspondence of historical authors.

We direct our attention to the 'marginal revolution', which changed the outlook of the Canon of economics until today. In his survey of the marginal revolution, Steedman (1997: 61–2) argues that abstractions made in the study of the history of economic thought may be useful, but cannot replace the lecture of original texts. In his case, reading the *Theory of Political Economy* reveals that Jevons' economics are a complex mixture of 'classical' and 'neo-classical' elements. We should take the *Theory of Political Economy* seriously. Jevons' economic thought stands on its own and should not be pressed into categories that are too narrow. In this chapter, we investigate the development of Jevons' deconstruction of the 'Ricardian' canon and the establishment of a new framework.

As indicated in Chapter 1, a fundamentally new aspect of Jevons' work is his attention devoted to the phenomenon of business cycles. The 'railway boom crisis' and the subsequent bankruptcy of the family firm were very influential in this respect. We can find traces of this crisis in his writings. In the *Theory*, he states that 'we often observe that there is abundance of capital to be had at low rates of interest, while there are also large numbers of artisans starving for want of employment' (Jevons 1871: 268). In the *Lectures*, we find the same argument: 'we know there is such a thing as depression of trade when the banks are overflowing with money but they can't get anybody to spend it' (Black 1977a: 62). In a letter to the Editor of *The Times*, dating from December 1866, Jevons elaborates on depressions: 'It is apparent that the price of bar iron was very high during the periods of years 1845, 1847, and 1853–7, when much capital was in course of investment in railway and other fixed works. The revulsions of both 1847 and 1857 were followed by considerable depressions of price' (Black 1977b: 142). In this quotation, explicit reference is made to the 'railway boom crisis', which affected Jevons' life drastically. The crisis partly motivated Jevons to accept a post as an assayer at the Australian Mint because the large salary would be of great assistance to the family (Könekamp 1972: 16–18; Schabas 1990: 13–14; Peart 1996a: 2).

During his stay in Australia, Jevons received the news of the sudden death of his father. His personal writings and correspondence suggest that this tragic event shifted Jevons' attention from the natural to the social sciences. A study of his diary reveals that, once in Australia, Jevons' spare time is filled with natural science and meteorological observations. The entry of 4 November 1855 exclusively concerns his work on botanics, natural philosophy, molecular philosophy and meteorology (Black and Könekamp 1972: 113–15). Schabas (1990: 15) states that Jevons' interest in economics did not arise from one day to another, and argues that this interest cannot be reduced to his reading about the railway controversy.[13] After the death of his father, 'Jevons found in the social sciences a means to vent his "love of man"' (Schabas 1990: 16). Before the death of his father, Jevons seems not to be very interested in economics; thereafter, his interest in the subject gradually increases.

We can illustrate this evolution through a study of Jevons' published diary and letters. On 6 January 1856, Jevons starts reading *The Wealth of Nations* but, on 21 January, he has still only read the very first chapters on 'value' (Black 1981: 115). At first, Jevons seems not to be very interested in the subject. On 14 February, he receives the news of the sudden death of his father, and he starts writing letters to Lucy and to Henrietta (Black 1973: 208–14). His thoughts are almost entirely concerned with the 'sad subject'. In his letter of 15 February, these thoughts are related to morals:

> What a pleasure it is to know that he received & read some letters of mine in Rome [where his father died], and how I could wish that those letters had been expressions of all the love I bore for him, & which, unlike the rest of you, I had no means of showing since I left but by letters or by actions that would prove it.
>
> One finds a trace of selfish feeling in these which are the first few thoughts that struck *me*, & would I dare say most others also for themselves. I feel quite conscious that I should be more pleased by knowing that I had pleased him, myself than that the same amount of pleasure had been given by others whom I ought in unselfishness to love & esteem before myself. This however is no more than takes place with all our thoughts & motives which never seem to spring from a perfectly pure source.
>
> (Black 1973: 212, original emphasis)

On 17 February, he rearranges the different letters he received from his father (Black and Könekamp 1972: 115–23). His reflections on selfishness, caused by the death of his father, lead him to read the novel of Bulwer-Lytton (finished on 29 July), and undoubtedly encourage him to visit Woolley's lecture (the week before 13 September).[14] The novel and the lecture are concerned with selfish motives and morals, a 'good' subject 'and of interest' to Jevons (Black 1973: 132).

His reflections on selfishness drove him towards the science concerned with selfish motives. Mirowski's (1989: 258–9) statement that Jevons' writings should be seen as 'direct extrapolations from the energetics movement of the later nineteenth century' is not very convincing. Jevons' references to the conservation of energy concern the physical properties that were understood well before 1860 (Peart 1996a: 40–1). Moreover, Jevons writes in August 1858 that he must give up physics (Black 1973: 334; Schabas 1990: 16). Instead, his interest in economics grows gradually. On 25 March, Jevons finishes reading *The Wealth of Nations* and, already in 1856, he plans to write a work on 'Formal Economics'. In 1857, Jevons reads the *Principles* of Mill (which he dislikes, because he reads many parts 'but carelessly');[15] he gets engaged in the Land and Railway Policy questions, purchases Lardner's *Railway Economy* and commences his reading of Malthus' *Population*, which he regards as a 'great & useful work', etc. (Black

1981: 115–19). Jevons' attention shifted to the study of economics as a 'sort of vague mathematics which calculates the causes and effects of man's industry, and shows how it may best be applied', as he states in a letter of February 1858 (Black 1973: 321).

Jevons depicts the economy as a mechanical system governed by objective psychological forces (pleasure and pain) and disturbed by outward events. The development of Jevons' thought can be seen as a quest for these outward events. In 1860, he commences a work on political economy, in which value is 'to be established on the basis of labour' (Black 1981: 120). Only two weeks later, he arrives at 'a true comprehension of *Value*' and drops the labour theory of value altogether (La Nauze 1953; White 1991b).

In 1864, Jevons is 'undertaking the Subject of the exhaustion of Coal in England', which he regards as 'a serious matter'. White (1991c) remarks that Jevons' theoretical works did not receive much attention, so he began to write on practical subjects. Indeed, Jevons states that 'A good publication on the subject would draw a good deal of attention' (Black 1977c: 52). Jevons is looking upon the coal issue as 'the coming question' (Black 1977c: 58). White also argues that Jevons used a 'Millian framework' in *The Coal Question* as an opportunist, because he rejected it earlier. *The Coal Question* makes some use of the Malthusian principle of population. The reference to a Malthusian 'geometrical increase' is made quite explicit in a letter from Jevons to Cairnes:

> A matter which has been taken most of my attention lately is the possible exhaustion of our Coal Mines. I have lately completed an essay directed to clearing up the popular ideas on the subject, and showing that it is physically impossible for our industrial progress to be long continued (a few generations) at our present rate of geometrical increase. The consequences must be of a serious character.
>
> (Black 1977c: 65)

Mill's optimism regarding the 'stationary state' disappears in Jevons, because the result of the coal question will be a large-scale emigration with negative, instead of zero, growth rates. Jevons' preoccupation in determining outward, external influences on the economic system is also visible in the establishment of his 'sunspot theory'. In 1875, Jevons feels uncomfortable with Mills' description of the cycles as caused by 'mood fluctuations' as such. Instead, Jevons seeks *external* or *outward* explanations, and finds them in his famous but often ridiculed 'sunspot theory' (Peart 1996b: 144–6). The similarity with *The Coal Question* is striking; both times it concerns an external engine responsible for economic development. After all, coal is nothing more than 'sunshine bottled up', as Jevons remarks in 1878: 'now it is among the mere common places of science that all the motions & energies of life, whether it be that of the windmill, the waterwheel, the steam engine, the beast of burden, or the human operative, are directly or indirectly derived from the sun' (Black 1981: 97).

Jevons' reading of the classics

Jevons (1871: 268–9) criticizes the classical wages fund theory:

> Another part of the current doctrine of Economics determines the rate of
> profit of capitalists in a very simple manner. The whole produce of industry
> must be divided into the portions paid as rent, taxes, profits and wages. We
> may exclude taxes as exceptional, and not very important. Rent may also
> be eliminated, for it is essentially variable, and is reduced to zero in the
> case of the poorest land cultivated. We thus arrive at the simple equation:
> Produce = profits + wages. A plain result also is drawn from the formula; for
> we are told that if wages rise profits must fall, and *vice versâ*. But such a doc-
> trine is radically fallacious; *it involves the attempt to determine two unknown
> quantities from one equation.*

According to White (1991b), the remaining output should be divided between
profits and wages, but the basic classical distribution framework is unsatisfactory
because the output level cannot be taken as exogenous in a value and distribution
theory. Therefore, White suggests that the two 'unknown quantities' are produce
and profits. One unknown quantity is certainly profits, because the equation mentioned should determine 'the rate of profits of capitalists'. However, wages are
not determined either. Jevons grants that 'if the produce be a fixed amount, then
if wages rise profits must fall, *and vice versâ*. Something might perhaps be made
of this doctrine if Ricardo's theory of a natural rate of wages, that which is just
sufficient to support the labourer, held true' (Jevons 1871: 269). The following
paragraph is concerned with the refutation of this 'Ricardian' doctrine. Jevons
therefore states that, *even with a given produce*, the equation is indeterminate,
because we cannot determine two unknown quantities (profits and wages) from
this one equation.

The 'mathematical functions' Jevons wanted to establish departed from the
labour of one labourer, working on a land with a given fertility. As the fertility of
the land is given and rent may be eliminated as a surplus that is reduced to zero
in the case of the poorest land cultivated, and because the labour of the individual
labourer forms the starting point of the analysis, we arrive at a relation between
individual labour, on the one hand, and the division of the produce of this labour
between wages and profits, on the other hand. Jevons directs his attention towards
the classical wages fund theory in order to determine the unknown quantity of
wages. The question to be answered becomes the determination of the wages
fund. Indeed, Jevons states:

> The whole question will consist in determining how much is appropriated
> for the purpose; for it certainly need not be the whole existing amount of
> circulating capital. Mill distinctly says, that because industry is limited by
> capital, we are not to infer that it always reaches that limit; and, as a matter
> of fact, we often observe that there is abundance of capital to be had at low

rates of interest, while there are also large numbers of artisans starving for want of employment.

(Jevons 1871: 268)

The equation 'Produce = profits + wages' is indeterminate, because the wages fund cannot be presupposed, and this is because past experience shows that 'capital may be laid by'. This insight can be traced back to the railway boom crisis. However, Jevons (1871: 271–3) still uses the wages fund theory, because it 'acts in a wholly temporary manner'. At first, the wages fund theory is in operation (the capitalist advances maintenance to the labourers) but, after a certain number of years, the conditions will be completely different. Capitalists will learn and change their investment decisions.

Peart (1996b) emphasizes the role of investment decisions and 'errors' in Jevons' economic thought. Although individuals are, on average, good decision-makers, there is certainly room for mistakes, and education is required in order to promote correct decisions. Capital may be laid by, and investment decisions may change over time because of outward events, insecurity and a lack of knowledge.

The deconstruction of the 'Ricardo–Mill' canon

The Theory of Political Economy forms the result of Jevons' reasoning. Its disappointing reception leads him to deconstruct the contemporary canon and to establish a new canon to found his work on. The reception of Jevons' economic theory is adequately described by Black (1962). His *Notice of a General Mathematical Theory of Political Economy*, read before Section F of the British Association at Cambridge in 1862, does not receive much attention. The first edition of *The Theory of Political Economy* gives rise to 'only a small trickle of correspondence', with Shadwell, Brewer and G. H. Darwin. In 1874–5, the *Theory* becomes known on the continent. Jevons exchanges ideas with continental economists such as Walras, d'Aulnis, Pierson and Falbe Hansen. This correspondence leads to an 'international alliance' of mathematical economists, as they promote and even translate each other's works. In this process, the prevailing canon becomes deconstructed, as all 'evil' Ricardian elements have to be eliminated, and new 'predecessors' are discovered and put into the limelight.

In his *Brief Account*, Jevons argues that Ricardo made an 'erroneous simplification [. . .] when he assumed that all labourers have a certain uniform power', and he quotes Mill's definition of capital and establishes a 'much simpler one' (Jevons 1866: 308, 311–12). However, it is remarkable that Jevons refers to Anderson's theory of rent and not to Ricardo's. In a letter to Foxwell in 1875, Jevons states that Ricardo does not have 'the slightest claim to the theory, as it was quite as well stated by Malthus if not by Anderson long before' (Black 1977b: 146). This priority claim can also be found in Mill's *Principles*: 'This is the theory of rent, first propounded at the end of the last century by Dr. Anderson, and which, neglected at the time, was almost simultaneously rediscovered, twenty years later, by Sir Edward West, Mr. Malthus, and Mr. Ricardo' (Mill 1848: 425). As Jevons read

Mill's *Principles* in 1857, it is probable that he found Anderson's claim on the rent theory in Mill, but Jevons seems to be more hostile about this priority claim.

Jevons did not like Mill's *Principles* very much, as he read 'many parts but carelessly and rapidly' (Black 1981: 117), but he had 'respect for Mill's straightforward & zealous character' (Black 1977b: 167). Jevons was opposed to the methods of the 'Ricardo–Mill' school, but his criticism was mainly directed towards the 'followers' of this school who were unwilling to consider alternative accounts of political economy. De Marchi (1973) argues that this 'unwillingness' is undeniable, but there was no monolithic 'Mill faction' that 'sought to influence appointments in a manner which suggests that they placed a man's orthodoxy above every other quality'. After all, Mill mentioned *The Coal Question* during a speech in the House of Commons, and Jevons wrote a letter to Mill to thank him for it; moreover, Mill recommended Jevons in a very positive testimonial (Black 1977c: 119, 94–5, 120). In the Preface to the first edition of the *Theory*, Jevons describes the generally accepted canon.

> I believe it is generally supposed that Adam Smith laid the foundations of this science; that Malthus, Anderson, and Senior added important doctrines; that Ricardo systematized the whole; and, finally, that Mr. J.S. Mill filled in the details and completely expounded this branch of knowledge.
>
> (Jevons 1871: v)

Jevons continues by questioning Mill's claim that 'our conception of Value is perfect and final', and he criticizes 'the so-called Wages Fund Theory' (see above) (Jevons 1871: vi). The refutation of the 'Ricardo–Mill school' amounts to the claim that it does not keep the complexities of the economic system in mind: labour cannot be treated as a homogeneous commodity bought up by capitalists; and the 'Ricardo–Mill' definition of 'capital' is inadequate as it neglects the possibility that 'capital may be laid by'. The starting point for economic analysis should be the individual, as a priori generalizations about 'the system' cannot be made any longer. This implies that the diversity of individuals is a fact to start with, and economic theory should form a mathematical system in which the diversities are equalized through the establishment of a rate of exchange. The 'Ricardo–Mill school', on the contrary, started with 'erroneous simplifications', which a priori equalized the differences by a reduction of complex to simple labour and through the existence of a natural wage rate.

Constructing the canon

The disappointing reception of Jevons' ideas provoked the establishment of more solid ground to rest his theory on: a new canon. In 1873, Jevons starts searching catalogues and bibliographies in order to find some previous attempts to apply mathematics to political economy, but without success (Black 1977b: 3). New 'forerunners' are discovered in the process of correspondence between the different members of the 'international alliance' of mathematical economists. The most interesting person is Gossen. On the 14 August 1878, Adamson writes to Jevons that he found a notice on Gossen's work in Gyula Kauntz's *Theorie und Geschichte der National-Ökonomie*. It took him some effort to find the book, but he finally succeeded. Adamson offers a brief abstract of this 'remarkable' work to Jevons (Black 1977b: 267–9). A week later, Jevons writes to his younger brother:

> Within the last few days I have had rather a disagreeable incident in the discovery, by Adamson of Owens College, of an unknown German book, by a man called Gossen, containing a theory of political economy apparently much like mine. There are, in fact, a whole series of books, hitherto quite unknown, even on the Continent, in which the principal ideas of my theory have been foreshadowed. I am, therefore, in the unfortunate position that the greater number of people think the theory nonsense, and do not understand it, and the rest discover that it is not new.
>
> (Black 1977b: 272)

Jevons informs T. E. C. Leslie about Gossen, as Leslie writes, on 28 August, that he does not know the book and that it is not mentioned in Roscher's work on the history of German political economy (Black 1977b: 272). A few days later, the same written conversation occurs between Jevons and Pierson (Black 1977b: 279–80). Jevons' unfortunate position described above is slightly changed, as the discovery of Gossen reinforces Jevons' claim that he developed a 'true theory' of political economy.

> A remarkable book by a German writer named Gossen, published at Brunswick in 1854 has just come to my knowledge for the first time. To a great extent it anticipates my Theory of Pol. Economy, but my want of knowledge of German prevented my ever hearing of the book before, nor do I find that any other economists are acquainted with it. The coincidence is however very remarkable as regards the results especially, & goes far to prove the truth of the theory.
>
> (Black 1977b: 279–80).

Jevons informs Walras of the existence of Gossen's book on 15 September (Black 1977b: 281–2). Walras replies that he will try to find a copy of it, and he plans to write an essay in order to 'révéler à ces Messieurs les allemands qui savent tout, un livre lumineux, publié chez eux et dont ils n'ont nulle connaissance' (Black 1977b: 289). Walras succeeds in finding a copy, describes the work as 'remarquable' and undertakes a translation, assisted by one of his colleagues (Black 1977d: 21). Jevons holds Gossen in the highest regard, as he plans to include 'the best abstract I can get of Gossen' in the second edition of his *Theory* (Black 1977d: 22). Indeed, in the Preface to this second edition, much attention is paid to Gossen's theory. Jevons states:

> Under such circumstances [the fact that Gossen did not attract any atten-

tion, even in Germany] it would have been far more probable that I should discover the theory of pleasure and pain, than that I should discover Gossen's book, and I have carefully pointed out, both in the first edition and in this, certain passages of Bentham, Senior, Jennings and other authors, from which my system was, more or less consciously, developed. I cannot claim to be totally indifferent to the rights of priority; and from the year 1862, when my theory was first published in brief outline, I have often pleased myself with the thought that it was at once a novel and an important theory. From what I have now stated in this preface it is evident that novelty can no longer be attributed to the leading features of the theory. Much is clearly due to Dupuit, and of the rest a great share must be assigned to Gossen. Regret may easily be swallowed up in satisfaction if I succeed eventually in making that understood and valued which has been so sadly neglected.

(Jevons 1871: xxxvii–xxxviii)

The unfortunate and discouraging aspect of the matter is the complete oblivion into which this part of the literature of Economics has always fallen, oblivion so complete that each mathematico-economic writer has been obliged to begin almost *de novo*. It is with the purpose of preventing for the future as far as I can such ignorance of previous exertions, that I have spent so much pains upon this list of books.

(Jevons 1871: xliii)

The new canon is ready: Ricardo and Mill 'shunted the car Economic science on to a wrong line', and previously unknown authors such as Gossen, Thünen, Cournot, Dupuit, etc. receive a proper place in this new construction.

When at length a true system of Economics comes to be established, it will be seen that that able but wrong-headed man, David Ricardo, shunted the car of Economic science on to a wrong line – a line, however, on which it was further urged towards confusion by his equally able and wrong-headed admirer, John Stuart Mill. There were Economists, such as Malthus and Senior, who had a far better comprehension of the true doctrines (though not free from the Ricardian errors), but they were driven out of the field by the unity and influence of the Ricardo–Mill school. It will be a work of labour to pick up the fragments of a shattered science and to start anew, but it is a work from which they must not shrink who wish to see any advance of Economic Science.

(Jevons 1871: li–lii)

Jevons does, however, retain the central position of Adam Smith, the 'founder of economic science', in his canon:

I am beginning to think very strongly that the true line of economic science descends from Smith through Malthus through Senior while another branch through Ricardo to Mill has put as much error into the science as they have truth.

(Black 1977b: 146)

Jevons is very favourable regarding *The Wealth of Nations*: he describes it as 'an excellent, though rather old book' (Black 1973: 280) and states that 'it contains probably more truth & less error than any other book on the same subject, altho' it still contains a considerable amount of error' (Black 1977a: 3). This opinion amounts to the claim that 'it is all in Adam Smith', a view which can also be found in Macleod (Black 1977b: 115–16). As the book 'still contains a considerable amount of error', it should be revised. Indeed, Jevons undertakes a project to write an 'abridged' edition of *The Wealth of Nations*, but he never completes it. In a letter to Macmillan, he states:

It seems to me that the Wealth of Nations particularly requires abridgment; it was from the first rather a collection of treatises and disgressions than a single connected whole, and large parts of the work are either obsolete or of inferior interest. [. . .] These notes [which would be mostly selected from the best writers on pol.econ.] would enable me to some extent to fill up the gaps in Smiths doctrines [. . .] I should endeavour to make the work neutral ground and while passing over doctrines which seem false, I would confine myself to presenting in the original language the best established facts of political economy.

(Black 1977b: 218–19)

Therefore, the new canon starts with a revised *Wealth of Nations* and descends from classical authors, clarified from 'Ricardian errors', and newly discovered mathematical economists to the 'international alliance of mathematical economists'. The newly discovered economists still have a place in the generally accepted canon: there is no text book on *The History of Political Economy* that does not mention Gossen.

However, the attempts to withdraw Ricardo from the canon failed, as he was 'picked' up again by authors such as Marshall, Clark, Walker and Hobson. Marshall states:

There are few writers of modern times who have approached as near to the brilliant originality of Ricardo as Jevons has done. But he appears to have judged both Ricardo and Mill harshly, and to have attributed to them doctrines narrower and less scientific than those which they really held.

(Marshall 1890: 673)

In the 1891 volume of *The Quarterly Journal of Economics*, three articles on 'Ricardian' rent by Clark, Hobson and Walker appeared. Explicit reference is made to Ricardo, but none to Jevons. Clark writes:

The law of rent has become an obstacle to scientific progress: it has retarded the attainment of a true theory of distribution. Yet it is itself capable of affording such a theory. The principle that has been made to govern the income derived from land actually governs those derived from capital and from labour. Interest as a whole is rent; and even wages as a whole are so. Both of these incomes are 'differential gains' and are gauged in amount by the Ricardian formula.

(Clark 1891: 289)

We repeat Jevons' statement on rent, which is very similar to Clark's, although Ricardo's name is not mentioned: 'I would especially mention the Theories of Population of Rent, the latter a theory of a distinctly mathematical character, which seems to give a clue to the correct mode of treating the whole science' (Jevons 1871: vi). Although the resemblance between Jevons and Clarke is striking, Clarke refers to Ricardo, but not to Jevons. This implies that Jevons' attempt to exclude Ricardo from the canon failed. However, the discovery of previously unknown authors, the most interesting person being Gossen, changed the outlook of the canon until today. A canon is de- and reconstructed by every generation. In Jevons' case, the deconstruction failed, and his reconstruction was absorbed by a new canon in which Ricardo and Mill were honoured for their contributions.

3   Jevons and statistics

Adolphe Quetelet and the average man[16]

Introduction

Jevons' use of statistics was inspired by Adolphe Quetelet's 'science of man' project. Porter (1985: 66) argues that Adolphe Quetelet (1796–1874) was important in the history of statistics for 'his role in the development of thinking about the probabilistic error function [. . .] The curve was a characteristic not of things in the world, but of the imperfection of measurement techniques or the inaccuracy of inference from phenomena that occur in finite numbers to their underlying causes'. Quetelet applied the probabilistic error function to natural variation, making the curve an attribute of nature itself. Mathematical statistics was already a well-developed science, but it had never really been applied to nature or society. Statistical journals published large series of numbers without any analysis. Courses in statistics existed at universities, but these consisted rather of geographical descriptions and elaborations about the ethnic, social and cultural characteristics of a certain population. Quetelet's *social physics* brought mathematical and descriptive statistics together and convinced many scholars that a mathematical analysis of man and society does make sense.

Herschel's review of Quetelet's work, published in 1835 in *The Athenaeum*, contributed to the spread of the 'average man' methodology. Herschel argued that Quetelet adopted the formation of tables of mortality, which was widely used in the establishment of life insurance policies, to analyse human faculties. Quetelet was 'probably' the first philosopher to attempt the calculation of moral qualities. 'The very phrase, "human nature", implies that there is a common nature to all, and distinct from that which exists in each individual, and such words as *dwarf, giant, precocity, genius, etc.*, implying exception, imply also a rule to which that exception refers'.

Quetelet has inspired many scholars, in a general sense, and convinced them to use statistical techniques to analyse society. For instance, Walras refers to Quetelet in his essay *De l'application des mathématiques à l'économie politique*, originally published in Italian in 1875. Walras (1875: 327–8) argues that statistics can and should be used in political economy, as soon as sufficiently constant regularities can be established, although these will never be as fixed as in the natural sciences ('une valeur d'application durable'). The scope of this chapter is restricted to the 'average man' in the narrow sense. We will discuss two streams of thought that elaborated on the application of the 'average man' in political economy. We confront Jevons' political economy with the writings of several members of the German historical school. Both Jevons and the German historical school embraced Quetelet's statistics but, whereas the former tried to apply the 'average man' directly to political economy, the latter were rather critical towards the 'overshooting' that arises from treating the study of society as a natural science.

Adolphe Quetelet (1796–1874)

Lambert Adolphe Jacques Quetelet was born in Gent, Belgium, on 22 February 1796.[17] He studied at the lycée in Gent, where he started teaching mathematics in 1815, at the age of 19. In 1819, he moved to the athenaeum in Brussels and, in the same year, he completed his dissertation (*De quibusdam locis geometricis, necnon de curva focal – Of some new properties of the focal distance and some other curves*). He became a member of the Royal Academy in 1820. He lectured at the museum for sciences and letters and at the Belgian Military School. His scientific research encompassed a wide range of different scientific disciplines: meteorology, astronomy, mathematics, statistics, demography, sociology, criminology and the history of science. He made significant contributions to scientific development, but he also wrote several monographs directed to the general public. He founded the Belgian Observatory, founded or co-founded several national and international statistical societies and scientific journals, and presided over the first series of the International Statistical Congresses. Bartier (1977) argues that Quetelet was a liberal and an anticlerical, but no atheist or materialist nor a socialist. In 1855, Quetelet suffered from apoplexy, which diminished but did not end his scientific activity. He died in Brussels on 17 February 1874. An impressive amount of correspondence survives and is kept in various archives.[18]

Quetelet's published work includes collected data on meteorological phenomena and on population. He developed his theory of the 'average man' in several monographs. We will devote our attention to: (1) his *Sur l'homme et le développement de ses facultés, ou essai de physique sociale*[19] (*Treatise on Man*, first published in 1835 in Paris, reprinted in 1836 in Brussels, translated into German in 1838, into English in 1842 and into Russian in 1865);[20] (2) his *Lettres à S.A.R. le duc régnant de Saxe-Cobourg et Gotha, sur la théorie des probabilités, appliquée aux sciences morales et politiques* (*Letters on Probability*, 1846, English translation 1849); and (3) *Du système social et des lois qui le régissent*, 1848. Later works do not contain fundamentally new ideas that are substantial for our purposes. The second edition of his *Treatise* (1869), entitled *Physique sociale ou essai sur le développement des facultés de l'homme* (*Physique Sociale*), is not very different from the first edition, and *Anthropométrie ou mesure des différentes facultés de l'homme*, 1871, is largely confined to the physical development of man.

The development of the 'average man'

In his introduction to *Sur l'homme*, Quetelet argues that the 'Science of Man' should devote attention to the 'numerical appreciation of the facts' related to physical and moral phenomena of mankind. As individual peculiarities are infinite, investigating the isolated individual would lead to a generalization of what is entirely accidental. The separation of constant causes and accidents can only be achieved when a sufficient number of observations have been collected. The same causes will then always lead to the same effects, implying that moral phenomena resemble physical phenomena when observed on a large scale. It would be possible to establish laws, but they would not be invariable, as they would change 'with the nature of the causes producing them'. Moreover, those laws would only be applicable to individuals within certain limits. The 'social body' is the object of the science of man, and not 'the peculiarities distinguishing the individuals composing it'. Only a few men of superior genius are able to alter society sensibly. Man is influenced by numerous causes, such as his organization, education or knowledge, means or wealth, institutions and local influences. Individuals exercise 'disturbing actions' or 'secular perturbations' upon their environments, the effects of which, however, arise very slowly. It would be necessary to abstract from these forces at first and return to them when sufficient data have been collected. This process would lead to the construction of the 'social man', a fictitious being, similar to the centre of gravity within natural objects. The 'science of man' should distinguish between what belongs to the 'equilibrium' of the system and what belongs to the 'movement' of the system, but the centre of gravity of the system and the direction of the movement remain unknown (Quetelet 1835: 29–49; 1842: 5–9). It is important to emphasize that Quetelet does not study distributions (as Galton, Pearson and others would do a few decades later), but outer limits and averages instead. Stigler (1986: 171–2) argues that, in the development of Quetelet's thought, a shift in emphasis can be observed from the outer limits within which the fictitious centre of gravity moves towards an investigation of the centre itself.

Sur l'homme starts with the physical characteristics of mankind and devotes special attention to rates of birth and death. Quetelet presents a considerable amount of statistical data, but his discussion of fundamental and accidental causes is not very convincing and gives a rather speculative impression. Porter (1986: 46) points out that Quetelet's empirical and theoretical work is largely unconnected. On the one hand, Quetelet collects and arranges an impressive amount of statistical data. On the other hand, he develops an 'extravagant system of metaphors' to link the social domain to the theories and mathematics of the natural sciences. Both Porter (1986) and Stigler (1986) show that Quetelet's data are not always very accurate – which is not surprising, as he was one of the pioneers of systematic data collection. Moreover, in his haste to get things published, he is not very critical towards his sources and hardly ever checks his calculations. Porter (1986: 55) argues that Quetelet's lasting contribution is more abstract, as he builds a case for concentrating on statistical information presented by a larger whole, instead of devoting attention to concrete causes of individual phenomena. This is especially important for social phenomena of a moral nature, such as crime. In his *Sur l'homme*, he introduces the notion 'propensity to crime' (*penchant au crime*) to discuss the probability that an individual will commit crime (taking the influence of season, climate, sex and age into account) (Quetelet 1835: 421; 1842: 82).

The goal of these investigations is to determine the 'average man', which should precede every other investigation of society. This average man would be specific to every individual nation and also to every individual historical epoch. Quetelet argues that there is evolution and development during the history of mankind but, at the same time, he maintains that all faculties that are not based on science remain essentially stationary. The factor of change is human intelligence. Intelligence is growing continuously, thereby triggering scientific development (which is obviously cumulative according to Quetelet). But there is more: all characteristics that are related to intelligence will therefore change as well; Quetelet makes explicit reference to both physiological and moral features. Examples include the statement that the facial structure of the 'Caucasian' looks most promising for high intelligence and the observation that the moral quality of 'courage' has become less important since ancient times (Quetelet 1842: 98, 100). Mankind is growing towards intellectual, physiological and moral perfection, and the 'average man' is the archetype of this perfection:

> I have said before, that the average man of any one period represents the type of development of human nature for that period; I have also said that the average man was always such as was conformable to and necessitated by time and place; that his qualities were developed in due proportion, in perfect harmony, alike removed from excess or defect of every kind, so that, in the circumstances in which he is found, he should be considered as the type of all which is beautiful – of all which is good.
>
> (Quetelet 1842: 100)

Not only does intelligence increase as the 'average man' grows up, the limits within which the different elements relating to man oscillate also get narrower (Quetelet 1842: 108). This implies that people become ever more indistinguishable in the course of history and that 'monstrosities', defined as everything that exceeds the observed limits, will disappear. Quetelet holds that 'great men' in every state of society (such as Pythagoras, Archimedes, Kepler and Newton) come very close to the ideal of the 'average man'. They impersonate the mind of the nation as nobody else does but, at the same time, they distinguish themselves from others because of their genius. Great men unify particularity and generality. This apparent contradiction does not seem to bother Quetelet at all. If the 'great man' really is the impersonation of the 'average man', how is it possible that he has a high level of 'particularity'? This particularity can only be seen as a collection of accidental features, which is opposed to the conception of the 'average man' as consisting of general features only. The equivalence between 'average' and 'perfect' seems, however, to be sensible in the context of medical science, where Quetelet finds inspiration to develop an analogy. The physician has an idea of what constitutes normal or perfect health, and individuals who exceed certain limits are considered unhealthy and are in need of treatment (Quetelet 1842: 99). But would the 'average man' not just have an average intelligence, making it therefore implausible to consider him as an ideal and certainly not as a genius?

These issues become more clarified in his *Letters on Probability* (Quetelet 1846: 59–63). In *Du système social*, Quetelet uses the concept *centre moral* (Quetelet 1848: 107). The average is then the natural state, and deviations in all possible directions should be considered harmful monstrosities as soon as they exceed certain limits. Quetelet distinguishes between a real average (*moyenne*) and an arithmetical average (*moyenne arithmétique*). Whereas the real average has an existence in reality, the arithmetical average is a number that refers to something fictional, averaging quantities over a group of homogeneous but clearly different objects. Averaging different measurements of the height of one particular house leads to the height of that particular house, a real average. Averaging different measurements of different houses in the same street leads to the height of a fictional house, an arithmetical average (Quetelet 1846: 64–9). The 'real average' in this example would gradually converge to the actual height of the house, and the deviations would tend to distribute themselves to the error law because they were accidental. Quetelet thought that all living human beings were 'flawed replicates of the average man' similar to urn drawings: 'every individual ball is either black or red, and cannot represent the true proportions in the urn, but over the long run, the small error generated by each drawing becomes significant, and the binomial, which governs the probability of the residual error, converges to the continuous error distribution. Quetelet's originality was not mathematical; it arose from his inclination to regard deviations from the mean height not as innate diversity, but as error' (Porter 1985: 68). Quetelet then applied the law of error universally, not only to physical but also to moral and intellectual laws. For instance, the distribution of *penchants* to crime over a population would conform to the error function. The latter could therefore serve as a definition of type (Porter 1985: 68).

A further example of arithmetical averages is Quetelet's discussion of the general rise in the price of corn between 1817 and 1842. Two conclusions arise from this discussion: first, money is progressively losing its value; second, the limits within which the corn price fluctuates become ever more narrow. Quetelet argues that narrower limits are beneficial and that sudden price changes should be avoided: a rising corn price leads to a higher rate of mortality, whereas a falling corn price is harmful for the producers. He is in favour of increased corn imports, but not, like Ricardo, because this would counteract the falling rate of profit, but simply because this would increase price stability and narrow the limits of price fluctuations. The fact that this process of narrowing can actually be observed in the statistical data from 1817 to 1842 is explained by increased knowledge, institutional wisdom and political calm (Quetelet 1846: 70–73).[21] The tendency to narrower limits, which is equivalent to the tendency to realize the 'arithmetical average', thereby transforming it into a 'real average', is thus a direct result of growing intelligence and the cumulative nature of science. Porter (1986: 46–9) argues convincingly that Quetelet prefers the 'mean' in social and political settings because this would resolve social conflicts, and that this preference can be explained by taking Quetelet's own experiences following the Belgian revolution of 1830 into account.[22]

In *Sur l'homme*, Quetelet emphasizes that a meaningful calculation of averages presupposes a large number of observations. Only then will the different 'accidents' cancel each other out. This process of statistical enquiry leads to the determination of definite causes that will lead to the same effects as long as the causes exist.[23] The relative stability of these causes over time is explained by the very little influence that individuals have to alter their environment and, even if they succeed, it takes much time before all effects become visible. Only a few men gifted with 'superior genius' can sensibly alter the social state, but even their influence is limited (Quetelet 1842: 6–7). But then, how can the existence of these men with 'superior genius' be reconciled with narrower limits and the equivalence between 'average' and 'perfect' man? One explanation could be that intelligence is neither measurable nor comparable, and that it therefore does not enter into the conception of the 'average man'. Although Quetelet does not develop a theory of the IQ, he does discuss the possibilities of measuring intelligence.[24] To solve the apparent contradiction encountered above, only one reasonable explanation seems possible: a person is a 'genius' because he resembles the 'average man' so closely, and precisely this recognition makes him an outstanding and therefore particular individual.[25] The process of narrower limits, accompanied by growing indistinguishability of individuals, should therefore lead to more genius in the population. This is everything but inconsistent with Quetelet's belief in growing intelligence and cumulative scientific development, as we discussed earlier. Quetelet must, however, have sensed that the concept of 'intelligence' caused a particular problem for his 'average man', as he wrote a (very short) chapter on 'intelligence' in his *Du système social* (1848). Here, he argues that intelligence is a combination of nature and nurture and that true genius can emerge only when both elements are unified. Most ordinary students know more about nature than Archimedes did, but this does not make them geniuses; and potential geniuses who do not receive adequate education will also not contribute to scientific development. The chapter confirms that Quetelet identifies degree of intelligence with degree of resemblance to the average man, as he expresses the hope that 'phrenology' will someday be able to measure intelligence directly (Quetelet 1848: 114–42). Intelligence then is similar to good health and stupidity equal to sickness. True genius can only emerge if someone with a high degree of resemblance to the 'average man' receives an adequate education, which may explain the scarcity of these beings. In any case, Quetelet's identification of average and ideal remains problematic, especially in the moral and intellectual spheres, as many subsequent critics of his theory will point out. It is also no surprise to see that most of the measurements he discusses relate to physiological aspects of the average man.

Quetelet's view on the development of civilization also implies that the ideal of the 'average man' would become approximated ever more closely as time goes by, thereby bringing him effectively into existence. The ontological position of the 'average man' is also strengthened when Quetelet observes that, in practice, it is often impossible to distinguish a 'real' from an 'arithmetical' average. If a not particularly highly skilled person were to perform 5738 different measurements of one and the same individual, the graphical representation of the data would look similar to the graphical representation of measurements of 5738 different individuals. According to Quetelet, this counts as evidence that we can really talk about a 'type' of man (Quetelet 1846: 133–8). Moreover, the number of people reaching or exceeding extraordinary limits – in his examination of body lengths – is so small that their probabilities can almost be neglected (Quetelet 1846: 149–56). Quetelet therefore feels confident with his 'type' of man. However, the 'type' differs from nation to nation, implying that there is no real universal average man: 'chaque race d'homme a son type particulier' (Quetelet 1846: 139–48). As argued before, Quetelet argued that the distribution of characteristics in individuals occurs according to the error curve, and that this allowed the definition of 'types' (Porter 1985).[26]

For Quetelet, the 'average man' is thus an ideal that should be approached as closely as possible. But it is also an empirical result, reached by averaging (a large number of) quantities observed in certain groups, thereby characterizing those groups with certain average physical and moral features or propensities. Those empirical results allow social scientists to compare different groups with each other, and also to establish relationships between specific magnitudes. Although Quetelet knows very well that it is not possible to derive conclusions from statistical laws for concrete individuals, some probabilistic relations may be established. For instance, the 'propensity to crime' reaches a maximum at the age of 25 years; it is four times higher for men than for women; and most crimes against people are committed in the summer (in the winter, most crimes are against properties) (Quetelet 1835: 484–6).

Despite his use of the concept 'social physics', Quetelet never developed a thorough theory of social forces, but rather a collection of speculative explanations for relationships between certain quantities. Later sociologists, such as Durkheim, were primarily interested in underlying social forces and therefore critical towards Quetelet and his 'average man' (Porter 1995: 21). Desrosières (1997) argues that Durkheim's work explains why Quetelet became forgotten after 1920 [together with criticisms such as Halbwachs (1913) and the *Methodenstreit* (see below), as well as the works of Galton, Pearson, Yule and Fisher, focusing on distributions rather than on averages].[27] He argues that, because of Durkheim, 'the statistical mean has been returned to the realm of methodological individualism, and the "collective type" is no longer assimilated into the "average type"' (Desrosières 1997: 184).[28] The 'collective type' would represent the ideal citizen, whereas the 'average type' would be the arithmetical result derived from egoistic individuals, implying that both should be seen as completely different. It is, however, beyond doubt that Quetelet and his 'average man' influenced nineteenth-century social science, and economics in particular, thoroughly.[29]

From 'average man' to 'trading body': William Stanley Jevons

Jevons was dissatisfied with classical political economy, as Ricardo and Mill 'shunted the car of Economic Science on to a wrong line', whereas authors such as Malthus and Senior had 'a far better comprehension of the true doctrines' (Jevons 1879a: lvii). Jevons would like to establish a new 'canon' of the history of economics, descending from a revised Adam Smith and moving through Malthus and Senior to the new generation of mathematical economists (see the previous chapter). It is quite remarkable that Malthus and Senior are precisely the ones that Quetelet corresponded with.

There are many similarities between Quetelet's and Jevons' backgrounds, and it is beyond doubt that Jevons knows the writings of Adolphe Quetelet very well and that his methodology is thoroughly influenced by the 'average man'.[30] On 2 August 1857, Jevons purchased Quetelet's *Treatise on Man* (1842). Almost exactly one year later, on 4 August 1858, he writes to his sister Henrietta that he is working on a project that looks very similar to Quetelet's 'science of man':

> It seems to me that *Man* is a subject as little understood now as the *Heavens* (Astronomy) were by the Ancients. Within the last hundred years, sciences almost innumerable have sprung up, but mostly devoted to physical Nature. Comparatively few have perceived that Human Nature may also be the subject of a science. It is indeed a many-sided subject. Religion, metaphysics, ethics, jurisprudence, political economy, politics, and even, medicine, art, poetry and many other studies all have man for the subject. But the social condition of man as influenced by the many internal and external circumstances is perhaps an indefinite but a wide and rich field for further research.
>
> (Black 1973: 335–6)

In another letter to his sister, dated 30 January 1859, he makes very clear that he is inspired by Quetelet:

> All the investigations of Social Science must proceed on the assumption that there are causes to make people good and bad, happy and miserable, rich and poor, as well as strong and feeble. It follows that each individual man must be a creature of *cause and effect*. This has indeed been argued by Quetelet, a German [sic], but requires yet to be more completely proved.
>
> (Black 1973: 361–2)

Although it is unclear why Jevons believes that Quetelet is German, it is clear that his 'science of man' project is inspired by his reading of the *Treatise on Man*.

In his *Principles of Science*, Jevons refers to Adolphe Quetelet several times.[31] He reports that the 'theory of comparative frequency of divergence from an average, was first adequately noticed by Quetelet' (Jevons 1874: 188), describes Quetelet's experiment on probability (Jevons 1874: 208) and elaborates on his 'law of error' (Jevons 1874: 378–85). All references are to Quetelet's *Letters on Probability*, including the one in the important sections on mean and average (Jevons 1874: 360–5). Jevons prefers the use of 'mean' when Quetelet's real average (*moyenne*) is concerned (the approximation of a definite existing quantity) and 'average' or 'fictitious mean' when an arithmetical average (*moyenne arithmétique*) is dealt with. The fictitious mean is important, as it allows us to 'conceive in a single result a multitude of details'. Jevons repeats Quetelet's example of the centre of gravity within a body and elaborates on the distinction between cases in which an invariable centre is present and those in which it is not.[32] In the second edition of his *Theory of Political Economy*, Jevons refers to his discussion of 'fictitious means' when he defines a 'trading body' (Jevons 1879a: 95–8): 'By a *trading body* I mean, in the most general manner, any body either of buyers or sellers [. . .] Every trading body is either an individual or an aggregate of individuals, and the law, in the case of the aggregate, must depend on the fulfilment of law in the individuals' (Jevons 1879a: 95–6). Jevons equates aggregate and average consumption: provided that the community under consideration is large enough, the average consumption of the aggregate community will vary continuously as a result of price changes, whereas individual behaviour is strongly affected by accidents. If the individuals had exactly the same features (those relevant for consumption), then the average laws of supply and demand would be equal to the conduct of every individual.[33] If, however, the 'powers, wants, habits, and possessions' of different people were widely different, then the average would not represent 'the character of any existing thing'. The accidents would cancel each other out, and a certain 'typical' consumer would emerge. Although this is clearly a case of a fictitious mean, it would not be less useful: 'the movements of trade and industry depend upon averages and aggregates, not upon the whim of individuals'.

Jevons thus recognizes that people are not homogeneous and that it would be wrong to create 'representative agents' depicting individual behaviour. In the case of large aggregates, however, disturbing causes would cancel each other out. Here, Jevons applies Quetelet's large number argument, and he extends it further to the idea that large trading bodies (or the economy as a whole) do not depend upon individual accidents. If, however, specific policy questions are at stake, the heterogeneity of different societal subgroups has to be accounted for. Jevons uses the concept of 'character' in order to bridge the gap between universal theory and the characteristics of specific subgroups in society (White 1994a, 1994b). White argues that Jevons' work was not directed to the explanation of the behaviour of specific individuals *per se*, unless these individuals were representative of all market participants of a certain uniform character. The science of economics deals with the lowest motives, and the *Theory* contains 'representative individuals', who behave in the way required by the *Theory*. All economic actors do not have to behave in exactly the same way, but disturbing causes would balance and, therefore, the 'representative individual' may be an appropriate model for the *Theory*.[34] However, the theory is indeterminate in cases where more information about 'character' is required. This issue is explored further in Chapter 5.

The average man and the German historical school

Quetelet's statistical works are also discussed by several members of the German historical school. Adolph Wagner's principal statistical work *Die Gesetzmässigkeit in den scheinbar willkührlichen menschlichen Handlungen vom Standpunkte der Statistik* (1864) devotes a lot of space to Quetelet, the 'first living statistician in Europe' (Wagner 1864: 6). Wagner embraces Quetelet's argument that moral laws become visible when a large number of observations have been taken into account, and that this does not conflict with the existence of individual free will (Wagner 1864: 7–10). Wagner insists that the statistical method is valid only when the numbers are derived from a group forming an organic whole.

> We must rather restrict ourselves to interconnected groups of people that, like the population of a town, a province, a state or a whole nation, form an *organically interconnected whole*, linked through numerous strings of material, spiritual and mental relations, and therefore consist of homogeneous parts.
>
> (Wagner 1864: 15)[35]

Like Quetelet, Wagner presupposes the existence of the 'type' and believes that the statistician can discover this 'type'. He emphasizes, however, that statistically established 'laws' are merely regularities that are established inductively, but justified deductively from the fundamental proposition that effects are proportional to causes. As numerous different causes are operating on society, regularities should be dealt with carefully. The regularity as such does not *explain* reality (Wagner 1864: 63–80).[36]

The German historical school does not categorically reject Adolphe Quetelet's conception of the 'average man'. Statistical methods are helpful when studying the historical development of the economy and society. Wagner (1864: XIII–XIV) argues that the aversion towards statistics results from insufficient 'sense of number' (*Zahlensinn*). This 'sense of number' is predominantly absent among women, poets and speculative scientists. Held (1867) argues that the followers of Quetelet's methodology are pursuing, in a more sophisticated quantitative manner, Adam Smith's original research programme. Held highlights the historical and institutional considerations in *The Wealth of Nations* to argue that Adam Smith was really a predecessor of the historical method in economics. He reproduces several quotations in which Smith discusses 'ordinary' features of labourers, which he seems to equate with 'average' characteristics. This leads Held to the conclusion that the 'proto-historical' Smith makes a more or less implicit use of Quetelet's 'average man'. Whereas Smith remained too silent about this conception, Quetelet exaggerated its use, which implies that the correct method of applying the 'average man' lies in between both authors. Held's criticism of Quetelet is directed to the latter's transmission of the 'average man' to larger communities and even humanity as a whole. Knapp's (1872) criticism is much more elaborate.[37] Knapp's general idea amounts to the claim that Quetelet simply transposes scientific principles from the natural sciences (astronomy in particular) to the realm of the social sciences. The 'average man' is a scientific construct that responds, through the principle of cause and effect, to quasi-physical forces enacting upon him. Specific historical circumstances and existing institutions are not taken into account by this approach, therefore making it inadequate for the study of society. The historical school therefore welcomes Quetelet and his statistics, as they are compatible with the empirical and inductive approach to economics, but condemns his 'overshooting', which arises from treating the study of society as a natural science through the application of the 'average man'.

Conclusion

Originally, the average man simply expressed numerical relationships between statistical data. Quetelet did not use the average man as a model to explain individual behaviour, but as a yardstick to measure deviations from this presupposed ideal.[38] The deviations should be minimized in order to promote stability and diminish monstrosities. Jevons argued that the aggregate and the average are the same. The aggregate could be treated as an individual, provided the 'character' of the individuals involved was taken into account. Jevons justified this 'empirical procedure' with the erroneous argument that disturbing causes would cancel each other out, which is nothing other than shifting from the normal distribution of errors towards the normal distribution of observations. Nineteenth-century economists such as Quetelet, Jevons and Wagner presuppose the existence of a specific 'type' for a certain group of individuals, and collect and analyse data to describe this 'type' in a quantitative manner. Whereas the German historical school embraced Quetelet's statistical methodology, they also warned that the 'average man' should not be treated as a mechanical entity, and that institutions must be taken into account. In this sense, the story of the 'average man' is still present in contemporary discussions between mainstream and heterodox economic theorists. The next chapter investigates the relationship between the 'average man' and Jevons' writings on logic.

4 Jevons and logic

The extent of meaning[39]

Introduction

William Stanley Jevons is generally recognized as a forerunner of modern economics and statistics, but his logic and philosophy of science are not mentioned very often. In this chapter, we argue that this may be explained by Jevons' somewhat contradictory position in the history of logic: he tries to found mathematics on logic, but his form of logic is inspired by the algebraic tradition of Boole and De Morgan. This contradiction results in Jevons' inability to establish a genuine definition of a 'unit'. Whereas Jevons is unable to found a truly unified science, he creates errors that remain visible within his mechanical system as a whole, especially in his economic theory.

In the second section, we provide an overview of Jevons' reductionist world view. According to Jevons, the laws of thought are concerned with detecting identity or similarity between certain objects of enquiry. A term is a name for a collection of objects, and it may be interpreted in two ways. Interpreted with regard to intention, a term is a group of qualities; interpreted with regard to extension, a term is a group of objects possessing those qualities. We argue that Jevons' system is comprehensible only when interpreted in terms of extent of meaning, and that it causes trouble when interpreted in terms of intent of meaning. Moreover, Jevons is unable to deal adequately with instances in which interpretation in terms of intent of meaning is required (as in the case of the theory of number). Jevons defines 'partial identity' (or class inclusion) as a correlation of a group of objects with part of another group. Jevons clearly states that the whole and part of a class are not identical, which implies that they may not be substitutes. Substantial and abstract terms are an exception, because these terms possess the quality of peculiar unity: parts and whole possess the same qualities in the first case, and it is impossible to draw a distinction between part and whole in the second. Jevons' intellectual programme is directed to the development of all possible instances of a general term, as shown in the construction of his 'logical abacus'. Terms should be transformed until they refer to one or more concrete objects, which illustrates Jevons' preoccupation towards interpretation in terms of extent of meaning. This programme results in the project of a unified science, in which logic forms the foundation for mathematics, and physics and economics are mathematical sciences. We demonstrate that this system fails because Jevons is unable to define the concept of a 'unit'.

In the third section, we relate the problems in Jevons' logic to his economic thought. The 'extent of meaning' causes trouble for Jevons' economic theory when he discusses aggregates of individuals. These are treated as individuals as well, because both individuals and classes of individuals belong to the class of 'trading bodies'. Jevons' conception of the 'fictitious mean' forms the erroneous tool in order to bridge the gap between individual and aggregate, or between extent and intent of meaning.

The fourth section argues that Jevons' economic system should also be understood in terms of extent of meaning. Whereas in his logic, all classes should be 'developed in extent' (transformed into a sum of concrete individuals that are only 'numerically different'), in economics, all causal explanations should refer to individual motive forces. The interpretation in extent of meaning implies that Jevons has severe difficulties when discussing 'average' or 'aggregate' concepts. We argue that Jevons developed his statistical methodology in order to fill the gap between extent and intent of meaning: in the aggregate, the 'disturbing causes' – the peculiarities of the individuals constituting the aggregate – balance.

We conclude that Jevons' position in the history of science is somewhat strange. He tried to establish a unified science, but his peculiar view on logic and mathematics prevented him from becoming a predecessor of logical positivism. Despite his contradictory conception of a 'unit', which remains visible within his economic theory, Jevons is still seen as a precursor of modern neo-classical economics. Moreover, Jevons developed some statistical tools in order to overcome the problems in his economic theory, and it is precisely these tools that are the most important contribution of Jevons: he is one of the first economists to apply statistical techniques to data.

Jevons' reductionist world view

Jevons' reductionist system is based on the laws of thought, which express the ability of mankind to discriminate, to detect identity and to store these findings into memory. Robertson (1876: 12) argues that Jevons passed very lightly over the question of whether the laws of thought are subjective or objective.[40] Indeed, Jevons states:

> that logic treats ultimately of thoughts and things, and immediately of the signs which stand for them. Signs, thoughts, and exterior objects may be regarded as parallel and analogous series of phenomena, and to treat any one of the three series is equivalent to treating either of the other series.
>
> (Jevons 1874: 9)

The laws of thought are concerned with the products of mental reasoning, which implies that they belong to the branch of psychology. On the other hand, the laws of thought form the preconditions of reasoning, which indicates that they have to be impressed upon the mind. The laws of thought are therefore derived empirically from nature. Logic is an objective science, as it deals with laws that are 'in the nature of thought and things'. Jevons refers to Leibniz's argument that we cannot prove the laws of thought because they form the preconditions of all reasoning, and to Hartley's statement that we either have to accept the laws of thought or there would be no certainty whatsoever (Jevons 1874: 8).

Jevons' position is normative: he argues that the laws of thought are part of an objectively existing logical world that cannot be fully grasped by the fallible and finite human mind (Jevons 1874: 694). The human mind can make mistakes during the process of reasoning. We can, however, discover wrong assertions only when we can distinguish them clearly from all other assertions, which is only possible when the laws of thought are objectively true (Jevons 1874: 6–9). Jevons seems to defend Descartes' (1637) view that everyone possesses the same faculty of reasoning, but not everyone always makes proper use of it. As mistakes in reasoning are always possible, our thoughts cannot be the criterion of truth, and the laws of thought govern the 'events of objective nature'.

The laws of thought deal with 'identity, sameness, similarity, likeness, resemblance, analogy, equivalence or equality apparent between two objects' (Jevons 1874: 1). A general analysis of human knowledge would then consist of pointing out the likeness of things (Black and Könekamp 1972: 179).

> Two objects are alike so far as when substituted one for another no alteration is produced, and *vice versâ* when no alteration is produced by the substitution.
>
> (Jevons 1874: 19)

Jevons identifies three different laws of thought: the law of identity states that a thing is identical with itself; the law of non-contradiction holds that a thing cannot both be and not be; and the law of duality asserts that a thing either possesses a given attribute or does not possess it (Jevons 1869: 111). These laws express the same truth. Jevons would like to reduce the laws of thought to one fundamental expression of truth, but he is unable to state the 'characters of identity and difference in less than the threefold formula' (Jevons 1874: 6). Symbolically, Jevons represents the laws as follows:

(1) $A = A$

(2) $Aa = 0$

(3) $A = AB \cdot | \cdot Ab$

Jevons writes a for the negation of A, and $\cdot | \cdot$ denotes the inclusive disjunction. The central role of 'similarity' or 'equality' in Jevons' system is demonstrated by the use of the controversial symbol '='. Jevons argues that there is a strong analogy between logical propositions and mathematical equations and, therefore, the same symbol should be applied in both cases (Jevons 1874: 17). On the other hand, the 'symbol $\cdot|\cdot$ is not identical with +, but is thus far analogous' (Jevons 1874: 161). The central principle is called substitution of similars: the process of reasoning is nothing other than the replacement of a term in a 'logical equation' by its equivalent. The implication of this procedure is that the Aristotelian terms 'subject' and 'predicate' become indistinguishable, convertible and therefore useless (Jevons 1869: 87). The symbols A and B refer to 'terms' or 'names', and 'are symbols for the same object or group of objects'; they 'represent a noun' and 'stand for undetermined or unknown things' (Jevons 1874: 13–16). Jevons' terms therefore represent two things at once: an abstract noun, on the one hand, and an undetermined object or class of objects, on the other hand. A class is a collection of objects, and a term is a name for a class. A name may denote some or more objects belonging to a class, or it may refer to certain common qualities possessed by those objects. 'The objects denoted form the *extent* of meaning of the term; the qualities implied form the *intent* of meaning' (Jevons 1874: 26). When adjectives are joined to a term, its intent of meaning increases, but its extent of meaning decreases because it refers to fewer objects than before.

These modes of interpretation are essential to Jevons' criticism of Boole's system: 'In his selective or class symbols, he [Boole] maintains the long standing confusion of quality and quantity thus x in his system means all things with the quality x, denoting the things in extension while connecting the quality in intension' (Grattan-Guinness 1991: 24). Boole denotes by 1 all things of every quality; thus x + (1–x) must make up 1. Multiplication (the logical 'and') of this expression of 1 with x leads to $x(x + 1–x) = x + x–x$. Boole would cross out one +x against –x, leaving x; but Jevons argues that $x + x = x$ (the 'law of unity'), which implies that x + x–x is really 0. According to Jevons, Boole's method is true only when he uses '1–x as the more qualitative contrary of x in intent of meaning only. The anomalies arise where 1–x is treated as the numerical complement of x in extent of meaning' (Grattan-Guinness 1991: 24). We can extend this statement towards the claim that the introduction of Jevons' law of unity $A \cdot|\cdot A = A$ allows the interpretation of terms in extent of meaning. Indeed, Jevons writes: 'In extent x + x means all x's added to all x's [. . .]' and if we 'take all the x's there can be no more left to add to them' (Grattan-Guinness 1991: 25). Jevons seems to forget that his 'law of unity' causes trouble when interpreted in terms of intent of meaning. Boole, obviously bored with Jevons' letters, writes: 'To be explicit, I now however reply, that it is not true that in Logic $x + x = x$ though it is true that $x + x = 0$ is equivalent to $x = 0$' (Grattan-Guinness 1991: 30). In his review of *The Principles of Science*, Robertson (1876: 21) was also highly critical towards Jevons' use of $\cdot|\cdot$ and =: 'Mr. Jevons is [. . .] anxious to extrude [the particular symbol +] from logic; but I do not see why it does not tell with equal force against the use of the symbol =, the true fount and origin of the evil against which he finds it thus necessary to protest'.

Jevons is unable to deal with instances in which interpretation in terms of intent of meaning is required. An example is Jevons' attempt to define 'number' through counting 'units' in space and time. When counting coins, every coin should receive a proper name: we should count C' + C" + C'" + C"" + ... The coins are equal to each other (they all belong to the class C); they are different only because they reside on different points in space. Before counting, we should reduce all identical alternatives but, if the objects differ only quantitatively, we have to know the concept of quantity first before we can isolate this 'quality'. Jevons tries to reach the notion of 'number' through counting 'units' in space or time. 'A unit is any object of thought which can be discriminated from every other object treated as a unit in the same problem' (Jevons 1874: 157). The concept of 'unit' encounters some severe difficulties, as Frege notes:

> Wenn wir mit 1 jeden der zu zählenden Gegenstände bezeichnen, so ist das ein Fehler, weil Verschiedenes dasselbe Zeichen erhält. Versehen wir die 1 mit unterscheidenden Strichen, so wird sie für die Arithmetik unbrauchbar.
>
> If we use 1 to stand for each of the objects to be numbered, we make the mistake of assigning the same symbol to different things. But if we provide the 1 with differentiating strokes, it becomes unusable for arithmetic.[41]
>
> (Frege 1884: 50, translated by J. L. Austin)

As Schabas (1990: 64) remarks, arithmetic is thereby derived in some mysterious way from the basic laws of logic. Jevons' defective approach gives rise to a symmetry between logic and mathematics, because he creates equations that have both a logical and a mathematical nature. Jevons defines (A) as the number of objects belonging to A and, if A = B, then it follows that (A) = (B) (Jevons 1874: 168–72). Jevons thus defines logic as an objective science resting upon the laws of thought, and bases mathematics (erroneously) on this logic. Jevons stresses the 'deep analogy' between mathematics and logic, but argues that logic forms the more fundamental science on which mathematics rests. We have to remark that Jevons (in contrast to Boole) wants to play down the use of algebra in logic. We return to this issue in the last section.

The fact that Jevons wants to minimize the role of algebra in logic may explain why his theory of number, which is closely related to his interpretation in terms of extent of meaning, remains underdeveloped. Jevons acknowledges that, whereas it is true in logic that $A \cdot | \cdot A = A$, it is absurd to say that, in arithmetic, $x + x = x$ (except when $x = 0$). According to Jevons, we already 'defined the units in one x as differing from those in the other' (Jevons 1874: 162). This is comprehensible only when interpreted in extent of meaning: 2 + 2 = 4 only because the first 2 and the second 2 denote different individuals; were they to denote the same individuals, 2 + 2 would equal 2. Jevons does not see that, when interpreted in intent of meaning, 2 + 2 always equals 4, whether the first 2 and the second 2 refer to the same individuals or not.

The 'extent of meaning' is also visible in Jevons' discussion of wholes and parts. Jevons defines class inclusion or 'partial identity' as a correlation of one group of individuals with part of another group. The statement that all mammals (A) are vertebrates (B) is expressed as A = AB. The subject A denotes exactly the same individuals as AB: individuals that are mammals, on the one hand, and individuals that are both vertebrates and mammals, on the other. This is not an equality between classes as such (in modern symbols); the equality holds true because both terms can be reduced to the same individuals. 'Cabinet Ministers are included almost always in the class Members of Parliament, because they are identical with some who sit in Parliament' (Jevons 1874: 40–2; Mays and Henry 1953: 169). The relation of whole and part is not one of identity: it is not permitted to transfer qualities from the whole to parts or vice versa. This does not apply to substantial and abstract terms: abstract terms, such as 'redness', and substantial terms, such as 'gold', possess the quality of absolute oneness. An abstract term is one and the same everywhere, and a substantial term refers to a substance that is one and the same everywhere. This implies that (in general) the qualities of a substance are present equally in parts and in the whole and, in the case of abstract terms, we cannot draw a distinction between parts and whole (Jevons 1874: 28–30).

Jevons wants to represent all propositions in the form of identities, including propositions concerning 'partial identity'.

> *Same parts samely related make same wholes*. If, for instance, exactly similar bricks and other materials be used to build two houses, and they be similarly placed in each house, the two houses must be similar. There are millions of cells in a human body, but if each cell of one person were represented by an exactly similar cell similarly placed in another body, the two persons would be indistinguishable, and would be only *numerically* different.
>
> (Jevons 1874: 19)

Number is simply another name for diversity; exact identity is unity; and with difference arises plurality (Jevons 1874: 157). Numerical (in)equality is therefore a special form of (in)equality, and quantity therefore a special quality. We can, however, define the special quality of 'quantity' only when we already possess the notion of quantity. Jevons therefore already presupposes the concept of number. We can relate this issue to Jevons' depiction of the fallible and finite human mind: man is 'logically weak' and has to count in time and space. Intellectual existences may be in neither space nor time, but we have to represent the terms in categories of space and time. Space is not a necessary form of thought (Kant), but an impediment to logical reasoning (Jevons 1874: 33–5, 769). A perfect intellect would therefore not need to count in space or time.

The 'extent of meaning' dominates Jevons' intellectual programme: 'Having given any series of propositions we must be prepared to develop deductively the whole meaning embodied in them, and the whole of the consequences which flow from them' (Jevons 1874: 12). He produces a table of permissible combinations of general terms, restricted to the conjunction: with n terms, 2^n possible combinations can be constructed, as each term can be either affirmative or negative. Using this method, he develops a 'logical abacus', which forms the starting point for later electronic analogues (Kneale and Kneale 1962: 420–2). Starting from some qualities A, B, C, [. . .], Jevons wants to 'fill up' logical space with all possibilities ABC, AB*c*, A*b*C, A*bc*, [. . .] and then cross out all combinations that refer to a non-existing (group of) individual(s). Jevons' logic is therefore not only an objective, but also a mechanical, science.

We conclude that Jevons' system is meaningful only when interpreted in terms of extent of meaning. A term denoting a quality should be reduced to a (group of) individual(s) possessing those qualities through 'deductive reasoning' in the form of the 'logical abacus'. Even the procedure of bifurcate classification should be formed on the principles of the logical alphabet. When dividing A into AB and A*b*, AB into ABC and AB*c*, and AB*c* into AB*c*D and AB*cd*, it may appear that only ABC, AB*c*D, AB*cd* and A*b* exist in reality. However, the combinations that are implied to be in reality are ABC*d*, AB*c*D, AB*cd* and A*bcd* . The bifurcate classification does not mention that ABCD, A*b*CD, A*b*C*d* and A*bc*D do not exist in nature (Jevons 1874: 696). Jevons therefore carries out the development of 'the whole of the consequences' to the letter.

Jevons' goal is the development of a 'natural classification', based on definitions in which the meaning of all the words employed is made clear. A natural system is distinguished from an arbitrary or artificial system only in degree: the natural classification would reveal more 'resemblances' than the artificial one. The method of classification is related to the goal of the investigation, but Jevons seems to argue that there really exists *one* natural classification:

> It is true that in the biological sciences there would be one arrangement of plants or animals which would be [. . .] in a certain sense natural, if it could be attained, [. . .] that *arrangement which would display the genealogical descent of every form from the original life germ.*
>
> (Jevons 1874: 679–80)

A '*summum genus*' does not exist in Jevons' system, because it is impossible to think of an object or class without simultaneously separating it from what is not that object or class. An '*infima species*' is reached in the process of deductive reasoning when we arrive 'at individual objects which are numerically distinct in the logical sense attributed to that expression in the chapter upon Number. Either, then, we must call the individual the *infima species* or allow that there is no such thing at all' (Jevons 1874: 701–2). The fallible and finite human mind, restricted to counting in space and time, cannot hope to reach an encompassing 'natural classification'. What would Jevons have said about contemporary computers? According to Mays and Henry (1953: 167), 'if Jevons were alive today it is unlikely that he would be surprised by modern digital computers and the arithmetical marvels which they perform'. When discussing induction as the inverse operation of deduction, Jevons (1874: 123) seems to hint at the late twentieth century: 'The work would probably occupy a good computer for many weeks, but it did not occupy me many minutes to multiply the factors together'.

Jevons' quest for a natural classification is accompanied by an attempt to establish a unified science. Physics as well as economics are mathematical in nature, because they deal with quantities. This does not mean that they are exact sciences – there is no such thing, except in a comparative sense. The 'exactness' of a science depends on our ability to bring all relevant data more or less precisely into account (which is only approximately possible). Nobody doubts that the tides obey some natural laws, but the complex contours of the seas do not allow numerical verification (Jevons 1871: 3–7). As Schabas (1990: xii) states, Jevons was a 'Pythagorean without the mysticism', in a 'world ruled by number' portrayed as a huge mechanical system. As logic is an objective and mechanical science, and mathematics is based on logic, and both economics and physics are mathematical sciences, all the branches mentioned are mechanical in nature. The 'substitution of similars' leads to a project of a unified science: 'The whole value of science consists in the power which it confers upon us of applying to one object the knowledge acquired from like objects' (Jevons 1874: 1). The detection of similarities gives rise to the discovery of an objectively existing Platonic world: 'The constituents of the globe, indeed, appear in almost endless combinations; but each combination bears its fixed character, and when resolved is found to be the compound of definite substances' (Jevons 1874: 2).

Jevons' ambitions are not restricted to the natural sciences. According to Jevons, economics deals with units of 'pleasures' and 'pains', which are difficult to conceive. But we can measure these units indirectly, as they prompt us to undertake actions such as buying, selling, borrowing, lending, labouring, resting, producing and consuming. Even a physicist cannot measure gravitation directly, only the amount of motion that it generates (Jevons 1871: 11). Jevons' conception of 'mechanical psychological forces' is similar to the conception of gravitational force in physics – an analogy he borrowed from Richard Jennings (White 1994c). Jevons' work contains a large number of these analogies, which accounts for his project of a unified science. Schabas (1990: 84–9) argues that Jevons' theory of exchange, expressed in objective market mechanisms, relies heavily upon analogies with the theory of the lever. Jevons wants to reduce the observable to a more fundamental material world, an aim of science expressed in his description of economics as 'the mechanics of utility and self-interest'.

Fixing the fictitious mean

In the previous chapter, we examined Quetelet's influence on Jevons' use of averages or means. Jevons (1874: 359–60) identifies three different significations of the 'mean'. The 'fictitious mean' is simply a representative number serving as a convenient mode of comparing data with other series of quantities. The fictitious mean or average does not refer to a natural quantity. The 'precise mean' is approximately free from disturbing causes and leads to a natural quantity; the 'probable mean' is more or less free from disturbing causes and also leads approximately to a natural quantity. Jevons argues that the disturbing causes would balance in the second case, whereas the third use of the mean depends on the theory of probability. 'Probability belongs wholly to the mind', or is 'good sense reduced to calculation'. Probability and chance do not exist in nature, but the fallible human mind is diluted with ignorance and has to quantify rational expectations by measuring the comparative amounts of knowledge and ignorance (Jevons 1874: 197–200). Jevons' scientific programme is directed to the establishment of a 'natural classification', in which the constituents of the world bear their fixed characters. The fallible human mind can never fully grasp this natural classification and, therefore, the theory of probability has an important place in science.

Whereas the precise and probable means refer to natural quantities, the fictitious mean or average does not represent a really existing quantity. But the average is 'of the highest scientific importance', because it enables us to simplify data. Jevons discusses the centre of gravity within a body, which can be represented by the behaviour of one 'heavy' point, and the poles of a magnet, which do not refer to the ends of the magnet nor to any fixed points within (Jevons 1874: 363–5).

The fictitious mean appears in Jevons' economic theory when he defines a 'trading body'. According to Jevons, a trading body is any body of either buyers or sellers, which may consist of a single individual or an aggregation of several individuals (the inhabitants of a specific country or continent or the members of a certain trade). The mechanical principles of exchange remain true in every case:

> We must use the expression with this wide meaning, because the principles of exchange are the same in nature, however wide or narrow may be the market considered. Every trading body is either an individual or an aggregate of individuals, and the law, in the case of the aggregate, must depend upon the fulfilment of law in the individuals.
>
> (Jevons 1871: 89)

A single individual does not vary his consumption by infinitesimal amounts according to each small change in price, but the aggregate will vary continuously. The laws of exchange are theoretically true in the case of the individual, and practically true in the case of the aggregate. Jevons remarks that the laws representing the conduct of an aggregate never exactly represent the conduct of a specific individual. Although this fictitious mean does not represent the character of an existing thing, average laws are useful 'for the movements of trade and industry depend upon averages and aggregates, not upon the whims of individuals' (Jevons 1871: 90).

As Schabas (1990: 93–4) remarks, the treatment of the simple case of two trading bodies is justified by referring to the same practice in physics, in which the 'three-bodies problem' has not been solved yet (Jevons 1874: 760). Another justification by analogy concerns the use of the fictitious mean: as the centre of gravity does not refer to a specific material point, the average member of a trading body does not refer to a specific individual. Jevons (1871: 89–90) clearly states that the principles will always remain the same but, because of the impossibility of bringing all individual motive forces into account in the case of large trading bodies, the laws of economics can be held to be 'practically true' by using the fictitious mean. The link with his general reductionist system is made explicit, as

Jevons refers in *The Theory of Political Economy* to his discussion of the 'fictitious mean' in *The Principles of Science* (1874: 363).

We conclude that the laws of exchange remain true in the case of aggregates because they hold true for the individuals that are part of the aggregate trading body. This explanation is closely related to Jevons' interpretation in terms of extent of meaning. A similarity between classes holds true only when they denote exactly the same individuals, and the exchange process between trading bodies follows the mechanics of utility and self-interest only when these mechanical laws are fulfilled in the several individuals constituting these trading bodies.

Jevons formalized the behaviour of two trading bodies. Suppose that the trade body A possesses the quantity a of corn, and that the trade body B possesses the quantity b of beef. After the exchange, A will hold a–x of corn and y of beef, and B will hold x of corn and b–y of beef. Jevons defines the final degree of utility as 'meaning the degree of utility of the last addition, or the next possible addition of a very small, or infinitely small, quantity to the existing stock' (Jevons 1871: 51). If the final degree of utility of corn is denoted by $\phi_1(a-x)$ for A and $\phi_2 x$ for B, and the final degree of utility of beef is represented by $\psi_1 y$ and $\psi_2(b-y)$ for A and B, respectively, then the quantities exchanged will satisfy two equations (Jevons 1871: 98–100):

$$\frac{\phi_1(a-x)}{\psi_1 y} = \frac{y}{x} = \frac{\phi_2 x}{\psi_2(b-y)}$$

These principles remain true whether the trading bodies under consideration consist of individuals or aggregates of individuals. In this last case, the 'aggregate' is the same as the 'average' (Jevons 1871: 89), which implies that the functions ϕ_1 and ψ_1 are the utility functions of both the aggregate and the average. As the behaviour of the aggregate is equal to the behaviour of the average, the individual peculiarities disappear in both cases, which implies that the 'disturbing' causes 'balance' (Peart 1995).

The Jevonian approach already came under criticism when Edgeworth (1881: 29) discovered that the outcome of the exchange process would be indeterminate in the absence of bargaining, as all the points on the contract curve would be possible solutions for the exchange equation.[42] Peach (1987) raises the more important criticism that estimation of the amount of utility by 'reading back' from its 'quantitative effects' expressed in actions cannot be carried out meaningfully without allowing interpersonal comparison of utility, a procedure forbidden by Jevons (Jevons 1871: 14). But elsewhere, Jevons explicitly compares the final degree of utility of money for poor and rich families (Jevons 1871: 140–1), and concludes that it is difficult to enquire about certain aggregate problems because of the 'vast differences in the condition of persons' (Jevons 1871: 148). We will not develop this already well-known criticism in further detail, but direct our attention to the connection with Jevons' general reductionist system.

By reducing the observable to a more fundamental world, Jevons assumes that every individual acts according to the same mechanical laws concerning utility and self-interest. The bargaining power is not taken into account in the discussion of trading bodies, the social positions of the different individuals disappear altogether and, most fundamentally, the different tastes and aspirations of individuals become equalized as they appear only as a 'fictitious mean' in the context of a large trading body.

We can relate this issue to Jevons' failure to provide an adequate theory of number. Counting $C + C + C + C + [...]$ does not provide an acceptable foundation, because we cannot discriminate between the different Cs. As in real life, where individuals are different, we should count $C' + C'' + C''' + C'''' + [...]$, but this is, as Frege notes, unusable in arithmetic theory. In physics, the mass points of a body are different only because they reside on different positions; the use of the 'fictitious mean' does not bear important ontological implications. If we apply the same principle to economic theory, we are in fact equalizing different individuals and hence creating a poor theoretical 'fundamental' world.

Jevons (1871: 93–5) states that his theory of exchange is concerned with static equilibrium analysis, but not with dynamics. Commodities are continually produced, exchanged and consumed; it should therefore be treated as a problem of dynamics.

> But it would surely be absurd to attempt the more difficult question when the more easy one is yet so imperfectly within our power. It is only as a purely statical problem that I can venture to treat the action of exchange. Holders of commodities will be regarded not as continuously passing on these commodities in streams of trade, but as possessing certain fixed amounts which they exchange until they come to equilibrium.
>
> (Jevons 1871: 93–5)

Once again, Jevons legitimizes this approach by referring to current practice in physics (Schabas 1990: 89–92). The analogy made here concerns the case of a moving pendulum:

> It is much more easy to determine the point at which a pendulum will come to rest than to calculate the velocity at which it will move when displaced from that point of rest. Just so, it is a far more easy task to lay down the conditions under which trade is completed and interchange ceases, than to attempt to ascertain at what rate trade will go on when equilibrium is not attained.
>
> (Jevons 1871: 94)

After having presented this analogy, Jevons goes on to develop his theory of exchange in which the simple case of two trading bodies is concerned. Owing to the substitution of similars, this approach holds true in the case of individuals as well as aggregates of individuals. But, once again, the analogy with the pendulum is deceptive: two mass points of the pendulum differ only in their position

– changing the position of these points will not alter the position at which the pendulum will come to rest. In large trading bodies, consisting of different individual persons, the positions of these individuals will certainly affect the outcome of the exchange process: as every individual in the trading body has his/her own tastes and aspirations, the relative position might have its influence on the equilibrium.

Suppose two countries A and B are involved in an exchange process. Country A is in possession of natural resources a, extraction of which would give rise to ecological or social problems. When the inhabitant of A leading the bargaining process prefers social and ecological stability to material values, the outcome might be that country B will have to offer more goods b in exchange for fewer goods a than otherwise. A relative change in the position of persons within the trading body will therefore have its effects on the equilibrium position, unlike the change in position of two mass points in the pendulum. In other words: 'disturbing causes' do not balance in the case of large trading bodies.[43] Hence, the static approach includes the concept of 'fictitious mean', which ignores the different persons involved in the trading body. The static approach thus reinforces our statement that, through the substitution of similars, individuals as well as classes become equalized in economic theory as well. If Jevons' system really would conform to real life, it would not only imply interpersonal comparison of utility structures, but also the real existence of a 'fictitious mean' incorporated in the person leading the bargaining process. The principle of marginal utility, derived from mechanical analogies of the pendulum or the lever, cannot be extended without problems to the case of trading bodies consisting of an aggregate of individuals, because the relative position of the individuals within the trading body has to be taken into account. The analogy with Jevons' unsuccessful 'theory of number' is once again striking. The gap between extent and intent of meaning cannot be filled by 'averaging out' 'disturbing causes'. As we have seen in the previous chapter, Jevons' justification of this approach is to be found in the 'large number argument' of Quetelet's 'science of man'.

Logical positivism, statistics and mathematical economics

Grattan-Guinness (1988) identifies two traditions in the interactions between mathematics and logics: the algebraic tradition includes Boole and De Morgan; the mathematical tradition includes Peano and Russell. Jevons remained within the algebraic tradition, but tried to reduce the role of algebra, whereas Boole gave mathematics priority over logic, as it should be used to analyse the laws of thought (Grattan-Guinness 1988: 75, 78). On the other hand, Russell tried to found mathematics on Peano's mathematical logic, but there is no connection between this tradition and Jevons' logic. Jevons tried to found mathematics on logic by using the concept of 'similarity' in his definition of a 'unit'. 'Boole used mathematics to analyse (his form) of logic; at the other extreme, Russell claimed that only (his form of) logic was needed to analyse mathematics' (Grattan-Guinness 1988: 78).

Jevons occupied a somewhat contradictory position in between these opposites: he tried to found mathematics on logic, but his form of logic was inspired by the works of Boole and De Morgan. It was based on the principle of 'substitution of similars', and Jevons was unable to establish a genuine definition of a 'unit', as Frege's criticism shows. Moreover, similarity as such does not provide a satisfactory explanation, as Hempel and Oppenheim note:

> The same point may be illustrated by reference to W. S. Jevons' view that every explanation consists in pointing out a resemblance between facts, and that in some cases this process may require no reference to laws at all and 'may involve nothing more than a single identity, as when we explain the appearance of shooting stars by showing that they are identical with portions of the comet'. But clearly, this identity does not provide an explanation of the phenomenon of shooting stars unless we presuppose the laws governing the development of heat and light as the effect of friction. The observation of similarities has explanatory value only if it involves at least tacit reference to general laws.
>
> Hempel and Oppenheim (1948: 323)

Jevons did not bridge the gap between particular entities and the abstract notion of number, or between particular facts and a general law.

The methodological proposals of Paul Samuelson (1963) in economics are very similar to Jevons' ideas. According to Samuelson, a theory should be identically equal to its empirical consequences. If A are the premises of a certain theory B, and C all the empirical consequences of B, then A, B and C express the same and are mutually interchangeable. If we start from some unrealistic premises A, we can never reach plausible empirical consequences C. As Machlup (1964) remarks, Samuelson drops all theory as a theory is always broader than all its consequences taken together (Mosselmans 1997a). Like Jevons, Samuelson does not succeed in bridging the gap between particular entities and general laws. We conclude that Jevons had a logical positivist *attitude* (the project of a unified science, the reduction of the laws of thought to one fundamental expression, logic as the base of knowledge), but he used a logic from the algebraic tradition, whereas a mathematical logic would be required.

Neurath (1983: 67) praises Jevons' mechanical logic: 'All this [physicalistical expression of equivalence] could be developed experimentally with the help of a "thinking machine" as suggested by Jevons. Syntax would be expressed by means of the construction of the machine, and through its use, logical mistakes would be avoided automatically. The machine would not be able to write the sentence: "two times red is hard".' On the other hand, Neurath (1970: 1–27) criticizes Jevons for not applying his reasonings to all the sciences: 'But neither Mill nor other thinkers of similar type [including Jevons] applied logical analysis consistently to the various sciences, thus attempting to make science a whole on a "logicalized" basis.' We argued above that this last statement does not do justice to Jevons' contribution to a 'logical' economic theory in which the extent of meaning is prevailing.

However, Jevons' main contributions to economics are his methodological proposals, which entailed the application of statistical techniques to the social sciences. Neurath (1987: 133) writes:

> Mill, Jevons, and Pearson were all very interested in the social sciences and tried to apply the empirical procedure to all questions without distinction. But none of these endeavours had the aim of making it possible for us to survey the wealth of our insight as a whole. Such a tendency is to be found in the pre-history of modern thought and is represented especially by the scholastics.

Contemporary statistical techniques were unavailable for Jevons, and most economic data resisted the application of statistics. Moreover, Jevons' conception of the fallible and finite human mind puts restraints on the possibility to 'survey the wealth of our insight as a whole'. Although Jevons' statistics were erroneous in certain aspects and did not succeed in bridging the gap between intent and extent of meaning, they formed the starting point for contemporary mathematical economics and econometrics (Morgan 1990: 18–39). Unlike Mill, Jevons did not devote much attention to 'disturbing causes'. His belief that they would balance was erroneous, but it made the application of statistics to the social sciences possible: 'As a statistician, Jevons played an important role in developing a conceptual approach to economic data that would later permit a quantification of uncertainty and the development of statistical laws for social science' (Stigler 1982: 364).

Conclusion

We conclude that Jevons combined a logical positivist attitude with an encompassing tension between the extent and the intent of meaning. Both his logic and his economic theory are comprehensible only when interpreted in terms of extent of meaning. Trouble arises when interpretation in terms of intent of meaning is required. The 'fictitious mean' (or Quetelet's 'average man') is an erroneous tool for resolving these problems, but it resulted in the application of statistical techniques to the social sciences.

5 Jevons and institutions

Bridging the gap between theory and practice[44]

Introduction

The previous chapters may suggest that there is no room for institutions in Jevons' thought, as the 'average man' is the focus of his attention. In this chapter, we examine the role of institutions in Jevons' political economy and relate this to contemporary discussions in institutionalism. Langlois (1986a: 2–5) emphasizes that the term 'new institutional economics' (NIE) may be misleading, because it suggests that this new brand is associated with the earlier institutionalism from the beginning of this century.[45] Although both streams share a common concern for the role of institutions in economics and argue that economics should become an evolutionary science, the ideas of new institutionalism merely reflect the opinions of the opponents of the earlier institutionalism. Although Thorstein Veblen, one of the most prominent members of the eclectic group of early institutionalism, used a humanistic rhetoric to criticize the hedonic psychology of the *homo economicus*, he did not substitute this notion for more realistic psychological assumptions. On the contrary, he adopted the psychological theory from materialistic behaviourism and wanted to clear economics from all kinds of human intelligence. Veblen was therefore unable to resolve the conflict between his humanistic ideal and his behaviourist psychology. New institutionalism relies upon one of Veblen's opponents, Carl Menger, who argued that institutions are in need of a theoretical explanation.

> The Problem with the Historical School and many of the early Institutionalists is that they wanted an economics without theory; the problem with many neoclassicists is that they wanted an economic theory without institutions; what we should really want is both institutions and theory – not only pure economic theory informed by the existence of specific institutions, but also an economic theory of institutions.
>
> (Langlois 1986a: 5)

Langlois' alternative programme includes situational analysis, which uses a kind of bounded rationality assumption in order to see the rationality or reasonability of human actions within a certain context. In particular, the role of institutions in the establishment of bounds should be taken into account. Invisible hand explanations are needed to show the emergence of economic phenomena as unintended results of human actions. 'Alternate compositional principles', such as selection processes, should also be studied, and the programme should finally be directed to an explanation of the emergence of social institutions (Langlois 1986b: 252–3).

Hodgson (1998) is highly critical of NIE and identifies some important problems for standard explanations of the emergence of institutions. The 'cultural determinists' overemphasize the role of institutions in the socialization of individuals. On the other hand, NIE focuses primarily on the emergence of institutions out of the interactions of given individuals. Whereas the first approach does not explain the emergence of institutions at all, the second methodology leads to a problem of infinite regress. For example, Williamson's (1981) transaction cost theory presumes the existence of the market in an original state of nature. Individuals operate in this given state and try to minimize transaction costs through the creation of specific institutions. However, Williamson does not recognize that a market is itself an institution, and that acting in a market presumes the existence of customs, habits, rules, norms, etc. These features should be seen as institutions as well. Hodgson argues that we are in need of an evolutionary theory that takes institutions seriously, and devotes much attention to processes of perception and learning. In particular, habits and rules should be studied extensively, as they are ubiquitous and cannot be answered completely in terms of optimization. Rather, contemporary evolutionary biology suggests that some basic cognitive processes precede the higher levels of deliberation, and are already present in higher animals other than mankind. Several cognitive processes therefore take place below the level of full deliberation and awareness (Hodgson 1998: 181–9). Hodgson (1993) argues that NIE still struggles with the problems that are associated with methodological individualism, and that a return to the 'old' institutionalism may therefore prove to be more helpful.

Jevons already struggled with the role of institutions in economic theory. We discuss several parts of Jevons' economic writings and relate them to the contemporary debates that Hodgson (1998) refers to. Our discussion will consist of three general parts. In the first part, we examine Jevons' conception of an economic agent and of the market. Jevons constructs 'representative agents' as individuals with optimizing behaviour, and defines a market as a 'non-institution', an unspecified medium of exchange that is not influenced by external causes. Aggregates of individuals are depicted as individuals as well, because Jevons believes that the 'disturbing causes' balance in his construction of the 'representative agent' (see the previous chapters). Although this approach amounts to a general negligence of the role of institutions, we show that Jevons does take the embedding of economic agents into account, especially in his applied economic work but also in his economic theory. Institutional settings are discussed especially in relation to market imperfections, and Jevons raises hands for the establishment of a science of 'economic forms and relations'. In the second section, we show that Jevons' assumptions regarding optimizing behaviour are subject to what he calls 'character', reflecting the class, gender or even race of the economic agent under consideration. Jevons takes rules and habits (and therefore institutions) seriously but, as he reasons from within a context of Victorian values and norms, which he does not question as such, his view on how institutions change is not very elaborate. Another instance of the role of institutions in his thought can be found in his emphasis on expectations and mistakes in the process of economic decision-making. In the third part, we show that Jevons puts much emphasis on the role of institutions for processes of learning and alteration of character and behaviour. Two different kinds of institutions exist: 'injurious institutions' prevent the market from reaching the optimal equilibrium, whereas other institutions may change the bad habits of lower class people and therefore facilitate the emergence of economic optimality. The creation of appropriate institutions may therefore give rise to a process of learning and cognition that leads the economy to a higher level.

We conclude that Jevons does not present a theory of institutions as such; institutions merely operate as a means to connect the notion of abstract individuals with particularities of a situation. In this sense, there is a similarity between NIE and Jevons' economics. Institutions bridge the gap between Jevons' theoretical and applied economic work, but there is no explicit discussion of the link between rational individuals and the creation of institutions. Rather, some Victorian values operate as 'hidden premises' behind Jevons' definitions. If habits (or institutions in general) really have their origins in pre-rational processes, then it becomes impossible to explain these habits in rational terms. Jevons does not try to explain institutions by individual rational behaviour, but would like to use some institutions to change behaviour in the direction shown by Victorian values.

Abstract markets and representative individuals

Jevons is often depicted as a mathematical, deductive economist who does not take the role of institutions into account. Margaret Schabas argues that Jevons tried to reduce the observable to a more fundamental material world. Market prices do not fluctuate around some natural or absolute value, but are derived directly from a series of fundamental motive forces. Jevons describes these motive forces as 'the mechanics of utility and self-interest', and asserts that prices are in direct proportion to the final degrees of utility (Schabas 1990: 84–9). Markets are then depicted in the most abstract fashion, and no reference to specific economic and social institutions is made in *The Theory of Political Economy*. Schabas recognizes that Jevons was not disinterested in these subjects, as is shown by his numerous publications on practical topics but, in *The Theory*, 'no attempt is made to specify a medium of exchange or to discuss the function of government' (Schabas 1990: 95).

It is, however, remarkable that *The Theory* includes a section on the definition of a market. Jevons writes:

In Economics we may usefully adopt this term with a clear and well-defined meaning. By a market I shall mean two or more persons dealing in two or more commodities, whose stocks of those commodities and intentions of exchanging are known to all. It is also essential that the ratio of exchange between any two persons should be known to all the others. It is only so far as this community of knowledge extends that the market extends.

(Jevons 1879a: 85–6)

Jevons' 'theoretical conception of a perfect market' includes perfect knowledge, individuals acting from a pure regard for their own interests and perfectly free competition. This theoretical market appears 'more or less' in reality, because the activities of brokers give rise to the establishment of a 'consensus'. Jevons raises hands for the publication of appropriate statistics, as this information would certainly foster the development of perfect knowledge among the consumers. This indicates that perfect knowledge is not necessarily a prerequisite for all markets, and Jevons mentions the example of a conspiracy of farmers withholding all corn from the market. A theoretical market should then be seen as an institution, which ensures that perfect knowledge is distributed among all participants at the exchange process. The interaction of brokers gives rise to the distribution of knowledge, which implies that the existence of these people in the market is a prerequisite for the market to be perfect.

Jevons does elaborate on an important institution, namely the market. Although it is merely defined as a non-institution (the absence of disturbing interference), some prerequisites are identified as well (a mechanism that ensures the diffusion of perfect knowledge and rational behaviour of 'representative' individuals). In particular, the attitude and behaviour of people should be kept in mind when studying concrete markets. Hodgson (1988: 172–6) argues that Jevons' definition of a market, like other earlier definitions, is much too vague. A genuine definition of a market should enclose the institutionalized mechanisms regarding the establishment of property rights, adjudication over contracts and transportation and communication of market-related information.[46] Jevons does however point in this direction with his emphasis on the necessity of means that would enable the distribution of knowledge (such as the publication of adequate statistics). Moreover, Jevons' concern for institutional settings in markets becomes visible in his discussion of 'impediments of exchange'. Here, Jevons supposes that the action of exchange cannot be carried out without trouble or cost, and he includes this cost as a variable in the exchange equation (Jevons 1879a: 106–8). This is not of course a theory of transaction costs, but it illustrates Jevons' view on institutions, which do not fundamentally alter the abstract conception of a market, but should nevertheless be taken into account. The same applies to speculation: it does not alter the laws of supply and demand, but thoroughly complicates the expected outcome. But this does not imply that we can simply neglect speculation, as 'the operation of law even among the most perplexing complications and apparent interruptions' should be studied if we really want a science of economics (Jevons 1879a: 111). Another place in *The Theory* at which institutions appear is in Jevons' discussion of bargaining: in reality, the motives and attitudes of the trading bodies influence the outcome thoroughly. Jevons mentions unequal amounts of knowledge among the trading bodies, their disposition and force of character, their comparative persistency, their experience in business, [. . .] (Jevons 1879a: 124–5). Jevons' definition of a market is indeed very vague, but *The Theory* also shows some concern for the conditions or institutional settings under which this somewhat taken for granted medium of exchange would fail to appear in practice. The market as such is depicted as an abstract ideal, and institutions may lead to deviations from this ideal.

This is especially visible in Jevons' discussion of credit institutions. Peart (1996a: 58) points to the importance of credit institutions in Jevons' theory of the business cycle. Credit institutions are important for the cycle because countries with institutions that give long credits suffer from crises more than other countries. There appears to be an annual cycle in the demand for money, with large withdrawals in the month of October. Jevons argues that the system of restricted issuing, as expressed in the Bank Acts of 1844 and 1845, is perfectly able to meet the problems caused by the annual cycle. The Bank of England has to discriminate between usual and abnormal fluctuations, and can take precautions beforehand. The Bank Act excludes only illegitimate expansion of the note currency, but preparations resulting from normal changes are allowed. Jevons therefore condemns the advocates of inconvertible currency or unrestricted issuing, because these systems would only enlarge the effects of the cycle and cause a general panic among the public (Jevons 1884: 151–74). Jevons' applied economics contains many references to institutions.

But *The Theory of Political Economy* contains, besides the definition of a market, several other instances that indicate that Jevons is not disinterested in the institutional setting of the economy. He seems to anticipate Hodgson's concerns when he argues (in the Preface to the second edition) that 'there must arise a science of the development of economic forms and relations'. Elsewhere, he even suggests that institutions have a life cycle:

> A HUMAN institution has, like man, its seven ages. In its infancy, unknown and unnoticed, it excites in youth some interest and surprise. Advancing towards manhood, everyone is forward in praising its usefulness. As it grows up and becomes established, the popular tone begins to change. Some people are unavoidably offended or actually injured by a new institution, and as it grows older and more powerful, these people become more numerous. In proportion to the success of an undertaking, will be the difficulties and jealousies which are encountered. It becomes the interest of certain persons to find out the weak points of the system, and turn them to their private advantage. Thus the institution reaches its critical age, which, safely surmounted, it progresses through a prosperous middle life to a venerable old age of infirmities and abuses, dying out in the form of a mere survival.
>
> (Jevons 1883: 82)

The establishment of a science of economic forms and relations should, however, be seen as a long-term goal for the science of economics, as the 'present chaotic state' of economics makes reconstruction and subdivision necessary. All these branches and subdivisions should, however, rely on certain general principles, and the goal of *The Theory* is the development of these general principles (Jevons 1879: xvi–xviii). We can assume that Jevons' proposed science of the 'development of economic forms and relations' should rest on these principles as well, although he does not state this explicitly. This implies that, although 'economic forms and relations' (or institutions) are the result of historical processes, the underlying general principles are not subject to change. This is certainly compatible with Jevons' general view of the world as a collection of fixed substances that are mixed up continuously (see the previous chapter).

Jevons' conception of a market should be seen as an example of those fixed principles, which however do not always occur in reality because of institutional settings. Especially the theory of pleasure and pain is subject to these institutional settings, as the 'character' of the person under consideration has to be taken into account. This is the subject of the next section.

Attitudes and behaviour in theory and practice

Langlois (1986a: 4–5) argues, as we have already seen, that Menger's conception of human nature is close to contemporary ideas in NEI. Moreover, he states that Veblen's criticism of marginalism is much more adequate in Jevons' and Walras' case. However, Peart (1998) argues that the economic decision-makers of both Menger and Jevons show some similarities, which should lead to the conclusion that there is compatibility between Jevons and NEI. Peart emphasizes that Walras' general equilibrium focus is absent in both Menger's and Jevons' writings. Although Jevons had some insights regarding interrelationships within the economy, he never focused on price determination as Walras did. On the contrary, Jevons tried to explain the act of exchange with given prices. His conception of a theoretically perfect market with trading bodies that show a price-taking behaviour allowed him to rule out situations in which no equilibrium could be attained as a result of non-economic factors (e.g. the impediments of exchange that we discussed above). Both Jevons and Menger devoted much attention to exchange behaviour (Peart 1998: 307–11).

Menger's conception of an economic agent shows great similarity to what Langlois described as a situational analysis with a certain bounded rationality. According to Menger, an economic agent has less than perfect information, operates under uncertainty and makes mistaken decisions. But this agent is also constantly trying to increase his knowledge about the world, and especially about the future, in order to increase the accuracy of his decisions. Menger argues that there is a difference between 'economic prices' and 'real world prices': whereas the former reflect the theoretical situation when prices are in accordance with the marginal utility valuations of the consumers, the latter are established because of mistaken valuations by the consumers. A similar picture emerges in Jevons' economic thought. Although the theory is based upon several main causes (e.g. self-interest), Jevons recognizes that, in reality, certain 'extraneous', 'capricious' or 'noxious' influences occur in the process of decision-making. Like Menger, Jevons argues that consumers tend to underestimate future consumption. Incorrect decisions occur, especially among the uneducated classes (Peart 1998: 312–19). The main difference between Menger and Jevons concerns the movement towards equilibrium: Menger states that consumers try to improve their decision-making abilities, whereas Jevons argues that this may be very difficult in the absence of education (Peart 1998: 320).

A perfectly rational human being would anticipate future feelings and include discounted future utility in his calculations. However, this ability varies according to certain circumstances, as there is 'the intellectual standing of the race, or the character of the individual' (Jevons 1879: 34). The ability of foresight depends on the state of civilisation: the class or race with the most foresight will work most for the future, because a powerful feeling for the future is the main incentive to industry and saving (Jevons 1879a: 35). Moreover, even the 'quality' of tastes increases with every improvement in civilization (Jevons 1879a: 40). Jevons' conception of an economic agent should therefore be altered according to the institutional setting in which the agent appears (in this case, the class or race to which the individual belongs). The influence of attitudes on the process of decision-making is also visible in several parts of Jevons' applied economic work. Sandra Peart (1996b: 144–51) shows that Jevons accepted Mills' idea that the fluctuation of 'commercial moods' would explain the occurrence of business cycles, but still maintained that these mood fluctuations require explanations themselves. Jevons derived his sunspot theory from his investigations, as he concluded that harvest cycles caused price fluctuations that were observed by investors and speculators. Time lags between expectation of economic performance and actual economic potential play an important role in the explanation of the cycle. Here, institutional settings do not seem to be essential, because people's behaviour is explained by external and non-economic causes (the harvest cycle). However, Peart shows that institutions may have a great influence on the process of decision-making: education could reduce the amount of incorrect expectations and therefore mistaken decisions. Peart elaborates on institutional settings that influence the behavioural pattern of labour supply as well, but we will return to this issue in the next section.

Peart's argument that mistaken decisions occur especially among the uneducated classes should be extended to an analysis of Jevons' use of the economic agent in different circumstances. Michael White elaborates on Jevons' use of the concepts of 'character' (White 1994b), 'gender' (White 1994a) and 'race' (White 1993, 1994c). White argues that Jevons' work was not directed to the explanation of the behaviour of specific individuals *per se*, unless these individuals were representative of all market participants of a certain uniform character. The science of economics deals with the lowest motives, and *The Theory* contains 'representative individuals', which behave in the way required by *The Theory*. All economic actors do not have to behave in exactly the same way, but disturbing causes would balance and, therefore, the 'representative individual' may be an appropriate model for *The Theory*. *The Theory* is, however, indeterminate in cases when more information is required. For example, it is unclear whether an increase in the real wage rate, proportionate to an increase in labour productivity, results in increased or reduced hours of work. More information about the 'character' of the person under consideration is required: whereas 'learned professionals' might be expected to work harder, 'lower class people' might prefer idleness over labour and prefer greater 'ease' in the case of rising real incomes.[47] The 'representative individual' of *The Theory* is linked to class and race behaviour by 'facts' expressing the 'character' of the class or race under consideration, and the Victorian middle class is used as a yardstick for evaluation (White 1994b).

Unlike Jevons' claim that 'mood fluctuations' are in need of further explanation, the characteristics of race, class and gender are simply taken as matters of fact. In particular, Irish labourers are said to be responsible for the higher mortality rates in several districts, because Jevons considered the Irish to be a race that would become more easily subject to drunkenness. He did not hesitate to manipulate statistics to prove his point (White 1993, 1994c). A similar picture emerges in Jevons' discussion of the reduction in working hours for women with young children. His ideas on this subject are gender biased, as he regarded the proper place of women as being in the home, and assumed that males make the labour supply decisions. Jevons concluded that women with children younger than three years should not be allowed to work, as this would only give rise to neglect of the children, and would encourage the males to choose idleness (White 1994a). In all these cases, the characters of labourers, Irish people or women are taken for granted, and are not in need of further explanation. Here, the attitudes and behaviour of people, considered as institutional settings, are simply given as external variables (which in fact belong to the domain of moral philosophy). Hodgson's criticism of methodological individualism is right to the point in this respect:

> Indeed, if we were to believe that action was entirely the result of constrained but otherwise free individual choices, then we may be quickly drawn to the conclusion that a great number of people are stupid, irrational, evil or insane. On the contrary, the institutionalist view leads us to emphasise that much of this behaviour is moulded by factors outside the individual concerned, and it leads to a greater respect for that person in his or her predicament, as well as a more fruitful and less simplistic explanation of those actions themselves.
>
> (Hodgson 1988: 72)

It is indeed the case that Jevons depicted lower class people as deviations from his rational economic agent in a bad sense. But, at the same time, Jevons argued that institutions, and especially education, may improve the 'character' of individuals. In the next section, we argue that institutions may influence the attitude and behaviour of economic agents in a positive, but also in a negative, sense.

Injurious institutions and the necessity of learning

Jevons devoted several surveys to the role of trade unions in the economy, which reflects his interest in the institutional setting of labour relations. His chapter on this subject in *The State in Relation to Labour* starts with what he conceives 'to be the true theory of the mechanics of production'. In the simple case when all elements of production (land, machinery, certain materials and labour by muscular force and mental skill and knowledge) all result from one person, no problem of distribution arises. In modern industry, the finished product is the joint product of certain requisites belonging to several different persons. Jevons argues that all agents are free to enter or leave a certain occupation, and that nobody can demand more than what was agreed upon when entering the occupation. If someone is dissatisfied, he can leave the trade at any time. The remaining partners have to find someone else for the performance of the same task, or they have to pay the dissatisfied person a larger share of the produce. Therefore, the remuneration of economic agents depends on demand and supply, on the question of whether substitutes for a specific kind of land or skill can be found in the market. Jevons repeats the 'law of indifference' in this context: like articles must be sold at the same prices when in competition with each other in the same market (Jevons 1882: 93–6).

Jevons answers the question whether a workman can claim any property rights in his skill, as a landowner can claim property rights in land. Jevons first anticipates the human capital theory when he argues that education and training are embodied in the workman, and that he may regard this as an investment that should be repaid to him by an annuity of higher wages during his lifetime. On the other hand, he states that labour 'is the primary possession of every person', which implies that the comparison with land 'necessarily limited and exclusive, each portion of each other portion', cannot make any sense. Except in a few cases (e.g. medical practitioners), trade monopolies are injurious for society: they privilege the few inside the monopoly, but they fail to secure the good of the people outside (Jevons 1882: 101–3). Jevons does not see that this criticism may be applied to the landowner as well. Jevons' argument relies upon the observation that everybody should be able to acquire a certain skill, whereas a certain piece of land can be appropriated only by one person or by one body of persons. The focus of his objective is quite clear: by establishing entry barriers, trade unions artificially limit the supply of a certain skill, and may therefore extract an additional scarcity rent that would disappear in the case of an entirely free market.

> Let it be understood, then, in the clearest way, that whosoever tries to raise his own wages by preventing other persons from working at his trade, and thus makes his own kind of labour scarce, attempts to levy contributions from other people.
>
> (Jevons 1882: 106)

Institutions are legitimate only if they alter human behaviour, in such a way that our precious resources would be used to improve our productive conditions. Public libraries, museums and public performances of music are especially suitable for this task (see Chapter 7).

Bowman (1997a,b) elaborates on the place of education in Jevons' political economy. He argues that classical political economy relied upon Malthusian principles to account for the influence of education on economic prosperity. Education would favour moral improvement and prudential restraint, which would lead to higher wages because of a diminished supply of labour and thus a reduction in the pressure on the wages fund. Jevons, on the contrary, focused primarily on improvements in economic decision-making: education would lead to more attention for the future and therefore to increased saving, and it would lead to less mistaken consumption decisions (e.g. diminished drunkenness). Moreover, both employers and labourers should be educated to see the benefits of co-operative production (see above). Jevons related education to labour productivity, and labourers are portrayed as individual decision-makers with various degrees of knowledge. Supply and demand determined the wage rate and, in the long run, everyone would be rewarded in accordance with his contribution ('residual rent theory').[48] Education may also be necessary to let labourers cope with business cycles: they should not spend their wages on alcohol and tobacco during a boom, but increase their savings in order to be prepared for possible unemployment after the boom.

Conclusion

At first sight, there seems to be no place for institutions in Jevons' theory. His abstract economic theory relies upon a few general principles: self-interest, maximizing behaviour, perfect knowledge, etc. Markets are depicted in an abstract fashion, and individuals are portrayed as mechanical entities. But this general framework consists of principles or laws that do not appear as such in reality, but only approximately. Jevons' programme for a subdivision of the science of economics should be kept in mind for an investigation of the role of institutions in his economics. His practical surveys show a lot of interest in institutions and, especially in his work on monetary economics, much space is devoted to an investigation of bank and credit institutions and their influence on the performance of the system. But *The Theory* contains some interest for institutions as well, as the medium of exchange is discussed in the context of impediments. These impediments lead to a deviation from the general principles, and should therefore be taken into account when studying concrete markets. Although Jevons argues that a science of the development of economic forms and relations is necessary, he does not have an economic theory of institutions in the sense of 'old' or 'new' institutionalism. Institutions serve merely as deviations from the ideal of the abstract market with perfect knowledge, and should be altered to ensure that the 'residual rent theory' would apply in practice. In particular, labour relations should be institutionalized in a co-operative sense. At this point, Jevons' theory should merely be seen as an abstract theory that is informed by the presence of institutions, although these institutions are investigated thoroughly in his practical surveys.

There is, however, more to say about this issue. Jevons' use of the concept of 'character' shows a real concern for the role of norms, habits and rules in economic decision-making. Here, we can see a compatibility with Langlois' concern for situational analysis with bounded rationality. But while NEI would try to study how these norms, habits and rules were established, Jevons simply takes them for granted. His framework of Victorian norms leads to a class-, gender- and even racially biased analysis. At the same time, Jevons devotes much attention to the alteration of the 'character', especially through education. This would lead to better consumption decisions, less drunkenness, enlarged savings, better forecasting of the effects of the business cycle, co-operative behaviour of employers and labourers, etc. A great concern for education forms a policy outcome of Jevons' approach. Another policy implication is a condemnation of 'harmful' activities by trade unions (e.g. monopolistic restrictions). Jevons does not therefore study the change in institutions (such as habits or norms) in a theoretical sense (which would be the object of NEI) but, rather, practical ways of altering these institutions. Jevons' approach also explains why his reflections on the role of institutions are not integrated thoroughly with his theoretical writings. Institutions alter the manner in which the theory would be applied in specific cases, but they do not fundamentally alter the theory itself. Moreover, several 'lacks' in his theory (e.g. the absence of a theory of the firm and of supply and demand curves) prevent his considerations regarding the role of education for productivity enhancement and labour supply and demand decisions becoming a part of the 'core' of his theory.

6   Jevons and religion
Unitarianism and evolutionism[49]

(with George D. Chryssides, University of Wolverhampton, UK)

Introduction

In recent years, the economics of William Stanley Jevons has attracted the attention of several historians of economic thought. Schabas (1990) investigated Jevons' mechanical economic theory and its relationship to his philosophy of science; Peart (1996b) put a stronger emphasis on Jevons' applied economics and economic policy; and other scholars such as White and Bowman published several contributions that investigate policy-related issues in Jevons' thought. This chapter would like to broaden our perspective on Jevons' economic thought by taking his religious background into account. Jevons had Unitarian roots, which seem to become less important in his later life, although he always insisted that he remained religious and tried to reconcile religion and science. Jevons' growing critical attitude in religious matters is reflected in the historical development of Unitarianism itself. One important historical factor in this development was the rise of evolutionist thought, which was generally embraced by Unitarians. Jevons welcomed Spencer's evolutionary thought.

This chapter is structured as follows. The second section summarizes the main content of Unitarianism. The third section investigates Jevons' religious thought and his interpretation of Unitarianism. The fourth section describes the Unitarian reception of evolutionary theory, Spencer's evolutionary thought and Jevons' reception of Spencer. The fifth section examines Jevons' writings on economic policy. Jevons refers to 'higher' motives to justify policy proposals that do not have a direct effect on the accumulation of wealth, but this 'hierarchy of motives' itself remains unjustified. This chapter represents this 'hierarchy' as an outcome of Jevons' interpretation of Unitarianism, held against the background of Spencer's evolutionary ethics. This does not, however, imply that Jevons' arguments are specifically Unitarian, and that non-Unitarians must necessarily end up with different views. This chapter merely suggests that, in Jevons' case, the origin of his 'hierarchy of motives' can be found in his approach to religion and science.

A brief history of Unitarianism

In order to assess the impact of Unitarian ideas on Jevons' thought, it is necessary to give some exposition of the history and principal ideas of Unitarianism. The movement has no single founder–leader and, hence, any account of its origins is to some degree arbitrary. In Britain, the British and Foreign Unitarian Association was formed in 1825, almost exactly half a century after the founding of the first British chapel to bear the name 'Unitarian': this was the Essex Street Chapel, established by Theophilus Lindsey (1723–1808) in 1774, aided by the celebrated scientist and theologian Joseph Priestley (1733–1804). The chapel was destroyed during World War Two by enemy action, but is now the site of the British Unitarian headquarters.

Unitarian ideas can be traced much earlier than the eighteenth century; indeed, the first recorded occurrence of the word 'Unitarian' was at the Diet of Lécfalva in Transylvania in 1600. The origins of Unitarianism stem from the Protestant Reformation and, in particular, from Eastern Europe. Three principal early reformers are identified as being at the forefront: Francis Dávid (Dávid Ferenc) (1510–1579) in Tranyslvania, Michael Servetus (1511–1553) in Switzerland and Faustus Socinus (1539–1604) in Poland. All three were non-Trinitarian in their theology, contending that the Trinity was contrary both to scripture and to reason. The 'father of Unitarianism' in Britain is generally held to be the English clergyman John Biddle (1616–1662), who spent much of his life in prison on account of his questioning of the Trinity doctrine. Although, in common with Dávid, Servetus and Socinus, he had difficulty in regarding Jesus as wholly divine, Biddle also contended that the Holy Spirit was a separate entity from the Father and the Son. Despite a brief reprieve under Oliver Cromwell in 1652, Biddle soon found himself back in prison after translating several Socinian writings and preparing a catechism – the 'Two-fold Catechism' – to rival the Larger and Shorter Catechisms of mainstream Protestantism. He died in prison in 1662.

The year 1662 witnessed another important event in Reformation history: the Act of Uniformity, passed by parliament at King Charles II's instigation, made compulsory the use of the Book of Common Prayer throughout England. The Act was unacceptable for Roman Catholics, Puritans, Presbyterians, Separatists or Independents and Baptists. About 1900 members of the clergy – tradition refers to the 'Two Thousand' – were forced to resign from their benefices. Most of them should be considered Presbyterian in sympathy; they were loyal to their voice of conscience and prepared to suffer for their beliefs. It was from some of these Presbyterians, together with some Independents and Congregationalists, that the British Unitarians emerged. The 1689 Toleration Act allowed Nonconformists (mostly Presbyterians) to establish their own religious institutions, but Roman Catholics and Unitarians were specifically excluded. This lasted until 1813, when the Trinitarian proviso in the Toleration Act was rescinded and, in 1828, the barring of non-Anglicans from public life came to an end (Wach 1991: 434). In 1825, when the British and Foreign Unitarian Association was formed, there were more than 250 congregations in Britain; by the end of the nineteenth century, this number had risen to 360. British Unitarianism was therefore flourishing, with a large membership, including many national and civic leaders, and high attendance.

Before the founding of the General Assembly in 1825, it is impossible to state unequivocally which congregations should be labelled 'Unitarian' or which prominent figures can legitimately be regarded as Unitarian. Competing groups of Dissenters had not much in common besides the Dissent itself. Social, institutional and intellectual historical developments explain why the Dissent was gradually transformed into a critical and rational approach towards religion, which led to the abandonment of a fixed doctrine in favour of a personal relationship between a rational human being and God. Altogether, three different strands of Unitarianism emerged from radical Protestantism: Eastern European, British and American.

The interaction between American and British Unitarianism can be seen in at least three areas: (1) the issue of doctrinal authority and, in particular, the relationship between reason and scripture; (2) attitudes to emergent scientific advance, especially evolutionary theory; and (3) the rise of the home missions and attitudes towards human need. The question of the relationship between reason and scripture is one that troubled Unitarians until the latter part of the nineteenth century. Until that time, it was generally assumed that one could give credence to scriptural authority, with the proviso that all scripture should be interpreted by the principles of human reason. One famous Unitarian exponent of this position was William Ellery Channing (1780–1842), to whom Jevons refers on several occasions (see below), who exerted considerable influence on important British Unitarians, most notably Martineau (see Holt 1938: 342; Webb 1992: 5).[50]

Channing was particularly renowned for his sermon 'Unitarian Christianity', delivered at the First Independent Church of Baltimore on 5 May 1819, which came to be known as the 'Baltimore Sermon'. After presenting a closely argued case regarding reason as the means by which the Bible should be interpreted, Channing argued that, although the Bible was self-consistent, not all parts were of equal importance. In particular, the New Testament was the culmination of the Old and, hence, greater emphasis was to be given to it, particularly to Jesus Christ, who was God's last revelation to humanity. Channing maintained that five doctrines, in particular, could be derived from scripture. First, God is a unity, not a Trinity. Second, Jesus is also a unity, not simultaneously divine and human or consisting of two parts: one human and one divine. Third, Channing affirmed the moral perfection of God: this implies love, justice and mercy, and divine mercy entails clemency for the penitent; the notion of eternal punishment is incompatible with such mercy. God wills the repentance of his creatures, and thus the world is a place of education, where one develops one's virtues, and thus salvation is by the development of one's character. The fourth principle concerned the 'spiritual deliverance' that Christ offers: in part, this entailed that Jesus was a moral exemplar to humankind, but Channing went further, claiming that there was an intrinsic connection between Christ's death and human forgiveness and that Christ's resurrection was 'the means of purifying the mind, of changing it into the likeness of his [Jesus'] celestial excellence'. Channing's fifth and final principle was Christian virtue or 'true holiness': one should act out of conscience, from a sense of duty. Moral character was therefore the principal quality to be valued, and Channing concluded the sermon with the following remark:

But we think, that religious warmth is only to be valued, when it springs naturally from an improved character, when it comes unforced [. . .] When we observe a fervour, called religious, in men whose general character expresses little refinement and elevation, and whose piety seems at war with reason, we pay it little respect.

(Channing 1819)

Channing's ideas mark a transition from a belief in biblical inerrancy to an acknowledgement of reason as the seat of authority in matters of doctrine. This transition was further assisted by James Martineau in Britain, who marked a watershed in British Unitarianism in his approach to scripture. Jevons had direct personal acquaintance with Martineau, having attended his lectures on moral philosophy in 1860. Martineau's substantial work, *The Seat of Authority in Religion* (1890), supported these recent innovations in biblical scholarship, and he argued that one could no longer assume a congruence between reason and scripture: the two frequently diverged, and it was incumbent on each individual to decide whether to follow reason or scripture. Unsurprisingly, Martineau chose reason for matters of doctrine, and conscience for matters of morals. His choice was generally endorsed by subsequent British Unitarians, and thus scripture was prised apart from reason.

Unitarians were not large in number, but very influential within the middle-class elite through several institutions. The Literary and Philosophical Society (established in 1781), the Royal Manchester Institution (1823, previously the Institution for the Encouragement of the Fine Arts), the Manchester Athenaeum (1835), the Mechanics' Institution (1824) and the *Manchester Guardian* (1821) are examples of institutions of an alternative liberal order that were dominated by Unitarian middle-class reformers.[51] Seed (1982) argues that the initiatives that originated from these people were not purely selfless, because they gave rise to prestige and authority (Bourdieu's symbolic capital). Scientific and cultural institutions and initiatives formed the backbone of liberal culture and the base for the exertion of political power by the middle class. The absence of similar Tory institutions explains why the liberal alliance remained hegemonic in Manchester in the 1830s and 1840s.

The rise of humanitarianism can be explained by the rise of competition. Rising competition, especially by small entrepreneurs, threatened the 'old capital', leading to the conclusion that these small companies were ill managed and that profits were made by mistreating workpeople. 'The intensification of competition in the 1830s thus produced a convergence between humanitarianism and economic interest among some of Manchester's largest cotton masters' (Seed 1982: 8).

Unitarians believed in science, rationality and education.[52] Education of the rational mind would reduce immorality and superstition. Unitarians contributed to university education, women's education, Sunday schools, night schools, day schools and adult education, because they wanted to free humankind from external authority and tried to foster independent judgement instead (Holt 1938: 20). The emphasis was thus laid on rational self-improvement but, from the 1830s, a more active interventionist strategy came to light.[53] This was marked, for example, by the 'domestic missions': such missions originated in the United States, and British Unitarians appropriated the idea in 1831, when the first 'domestic missionary' was appointed; the first Unitarian domestic mission was opened in 1835. Although the domestic missions were initially perceived as a means of spreading the Unitarian message to the unchurched, Unitarians soon recognized the social concerns that needed to be addressed. Education is useless when the first necessaries of life are still out of reach. James Kitson (1807–1885), for example, gave lectures on hygiene to working women in Leeds, and the missions encouraged savings schemes, clothing clubs and libraries.

Domesticity received considerable emphasis. John James Tayler, Minister of the Mosley Street Chapel in Manchester, used hierarchies of class and gender in his rhetoric of domesticity. Women's factory work should be seen as a violation of the domestic order and as morally harmful. Educating the children is of highest importance, as they should absorb conceptions of hierarchy, duty and order; the women had to make sure that regularity, thrift, moderation and religious piety were primordial in domestic economies. This gave rise to a tension between the private sphere (individual self-improvement) and the public sphere (active interventionism). Samuel Smiles (1812–1904), a Unitarian renown for his *Self Help* (published in 1859) and other writings stressing self-improvement, was against the trend; Unitarians were more inclined to offer external help with the social conditions of the late nineteenth century.

External authority had been replaced by the judgement of rational human beings. This also implied that, within the community of Unitarians, divergent opinions could exist and that several issues *were* debated thoroughly. One important instance of debate was the legal limitation of the hours of work by adults in factories: here, a struggle existed between humanitarian ideals, on the one hand, and 'scientific truth', as expressed in classical political economy, on the other hand. Most Unitarians active in the industry opposed the Factory Acts, but the 'non-manufacturing Unitarians' were severely divided. Another point of disagreement concerned the attitude to state aid for denominationally controlled schools. Unitarians agreed on other issues, for instance on free trade and on the repeal of the Corn Laws. Many Unitarians were also involved in the co-operative movement as a means of encouraging self-help and independence (Holt 1938: 25–6, 179–202, 258–62).

Some remarks are needed regarding the connection between Unitarianism and utilitarianism. There existed some close connections between Bentham and the Unitarians – some personal and some intellectual. Holt (1938: 26–7, 82, 169–72) regards Bentham as a Unitarian in theology, although he was not a worshipping Unitarian.[54] Bentham's 'greatest happiness of the greatest number' principle was suggested to him by a passage in Joseph Priestley's *Essay on the First Principles of Government* (1768). Bowring, a prominent Unitarian layman, was a close friend of Bentham and edited his works. Thomas Southwood Smith (1788–1861), who was a celebrated physician, reformer of public health and hygiene and a Unitarian minister, helped Bentham to write his constitutional code in 1830. The relationship between the two men was such that Bentham bequeathed his body to Smith for public dissection, in the belief that dissection of corpses was necessary for the improvement of medical knowledge and the discovery of causes of death. At the time, there was much public prejudice against the practice, which Bentham and Smith sought to counter.

Some commentators have suggested affinities between the ideas of the two movements. Thus, Mineka (1944: 145–8) argues that there existed a close connection between the economic, social and political ideas of Unitarianism and utilitarianism. Both approaches, he argues, are rationalist, and both movements place a high value on science and scientific method, and both display humanitarianism. However, James Martineau, in his *The Seat of Authority in Religion*, argued that Unitarianism and utilitarianism professed two distinct sources of authority, and that it was only through conscience that the springs of action (motives) could arise, and virtues such as compassion and beneficence find expression. Conscience, however, needs guidance. Conscience may tell us that we should give to the poor, but does this mean that we should offer money to anyone who begs? We can only reach a decision by considering the exterior consequences, and the principle of utility enables this. Martineau writes: 'If Conscience selects the right affection, Utility determines the fitting action; nor, without consulting it, is there any guarantee against the perpetration of well-intended mischiefs, which may bring the purest impulses into contempt' (Martineau 1890: 81).

For the purposes of our present discussion, it is unnecessary to discuss how present-day Unitarianism has advanced beyond such ideas. It is sufficient to note that Jevons' ideas are set within this framework of Unitarianism, which tended to see Jesus' work primarily as a teacher and exemplar (although not exclusively so), and which emphasized the importance of reason, unimpeded intellectual enquiry, education and an emphasis on conscience that gave rise to a variety of humanitarian concerns. Additionally, the belief in the intrinsic worth of the individual, coupled with a belief in the perfectibility (or at least the improvement) of humanity – a belief that was encouraged by evolutionary ideas in the nineteenth and early twentieth centuries – gave rise to the desire to improve fellow human beings intellectually and materially. Finally, both utilitarianism and Unitarianism recruited their members from the same social layer, namely the successful enterprising middle class. Jevons and his family belonged to this group.

Unitarianism according to Jevons

Unitarianism flourished, especially in Liverpool, where Jevons was born in 1835. His grandfather, William Roscoe, became a Member of Parliament in 1806. His support for the abolition of the slave trade cost him his seat at the next election, because Liverpool made big profits out of the slave trade (Holt 1938: 236). Both Jevons' parents were Unitarians, and his Uncle William was a Unitarian minister for a time (Könekamp 1972: 2–3).[55] William Stanley's journal shows that his interest in religious subjects dates at least from his adolescence. He seems to be inspired by his reading of William Ellery Channing (Black and Könekamp 1972: 99). He reports in his journal that he studied the Gospels in 1850 (when he was 15 years old), and he even started writing a 'rigorous history of Christ'. He took notes on the facts that were reported in the Gospels, compared them and arranged them in chronological order. Although Jevons states that this task was too difficult for his 'then powers', it indicates his critical and rational approach to religious subjects and texts. In 1862, Jevons notes that 'it is amusing to look back on times when I reverenced Christianity like most others' (Black and Könekamp 1972: 99). Jevons identifies two different approaches to (Christian) religion, which he attributes, respectively, to his eldest sister Lucy and his father Thomas. Lucy's faith relies on 'more concentrated and defined opinions' and is less grounded in reason, but it may be more intense and delightful than if achieved by doubt and enquiry (Black 1973: 225, 327, 337). Thomas Jevons' religious thought is described as 'liberal and charitable', and Jevons recognizes the same attitude in his opinions (and, although to a somewhat lesser extent, in the ideas of his youngest sister Henrietta) (Black 1973: 225). Jevons writes that, until 1851, he said his prayers 'like any good church-person', and then his conviction grew that his task consisted of increasing his knowledge (Black and Könekamp 1972: 100–1). Jevons' reflections on religion are intensified after the death of his father, and many thoughts are expressed in his correspondence with Henrietta, which dates from the time that he spent in Australia (1854–1859). His critical attitude towards religious subjects is similar to the thoughts that Channing expressed in his lecture. In 1857, Jevons writes in his journal:

> I was brought up in perfect freedom of opinion for though I can remember my mother teaching me my prayers, I was then very young, and what religion I have since been taught at school or elsewhere only led me to enquire whether the whole was true.
>
> (Black and Könekamp 1972: 154)

Although Jevons does not explicitly discuss the Trinity, it is clear that he believes in the existence of one God. He does not describe him as a personal being or father, but as a general principle of abstract goodness (Black 1973: 258). This abstract principle is in perfect accordance with scientific findings: he reports that his conception of God is derived from an examination of matter and mind. The world is a 'vast organism' with order and form expressing intention and mind, which implies that God is inseparable from his works. He is visible 'in the wonderful order and simplicity of Nature, in the adaptation of means to ends, and in the creation of man to which everything refers, with power capable of indefinite improvement' (Black and Könekamp 1972: 155). Jevons founds his faith 'on Man and his feelings', because humanity's mental feelings of love and sympathy are the only places where intentions of good can be discovered (Black and Könekamp 1972: 154, note 3). Every religion refers to the same eternal principles or 'moral truths', but the state of civilization determines their degree of misrepresentation.

Different religions are merely costumes thrown over these principles, and Unitarianism contains the 'most simple and truth-like' set of religious beliefs (Black 1973: 225–65):

> God is but the embodiment of the first and greatest principle of the world, viz., universal good, order tending towards good, design, all coming under the comprehensive term Providence, and Christ I conceive to be an example of a Perfect Man, and of the relation which such a character must bear to God.
>
> (Black 1973: 226)

God is depicted as a principle of abstract goodness, and Jesus is seen as the messenger who brought the eternal moral truths to humankind. Whereas Newton was a genius of natural science and Mozart of music, Jesus was a moral genius (Black and Könekamp 1972: 155). Jevons' views on religion are in accordance with the principles that are expressed in Channing's lecture: the existence of one God, the belief in Christ as a distinct person, God's moral perfection and Jesus' role as a moral teacher. Jevons emphasizes the moral perfection of God and depicts him as an abstract principle of goodness. Even more important is Channing's fifth principle: all virtue is derived from the moral nature of humanity, and religious worship is worthless if not accompanied by good moral conduct in daily life. Jevons writes about the Roman Catholic religion in Latin America:

> Catholic religion, imported from Spain here, gained vast power, wealth, and extension among a population formed to a great extent of native Indians, low in the scale of intelligence, and of negroes who are worse. As a consequence the religion became debased into something which I can only regard as a bad form of idolatry.[56]
>
> (Black 1973: 378)

Jevons is offended by the elaborate ritual and religious paraphernalia and, elsewhere, he even writes that Catholicism is 'very disgusting and only better than irreligion' (Black 1973:277). In a letter to Henrietta, he states that his only guides are truth and goodness. A good character follows principles of truthfulness and 'honesty of purpose', which means that he has 'a real regard for the good of others as well as oneself'. He therefore condemns all religions that teach sublime principles but perform otherwise in daily practice. Unitarianism, on the contrary, does not teach any creed, but only to be 'good and principled'. This may be too 'indefinite and uninviting' for most minds, but Jevons does not see other valuable possibilities. Humans should be judged by their acts, but these acts should also express principles of truth and goodness (Black 1973: 241–2). A religion should be judged by the amount of 'abstract morality' that it contains and by 'its effect on the character, condition and happiness of men' (Black 1973: 296).

Elsewhere, Jevons writes to Henrietta that she might mistake him for an atheist. He does not have the love for God because he is incapable of forming an adequate image of the Creator; but he almost deifies the 'Love of Man' (Black 1973: 326). This does not imply atheism because Jevons believes that God created the human mind, and that human feelings of love and goodness are derived from God's eternal moral truths. This leads, however, to an even stronger emphasis on reason and humanity than we found in Channing's lecture. Although Jevons writes that his religious convictions are not perfectly clear (Black 1977b: 36), his scattered remarks on this topic enable us to form a more or less consistent conception of his ideas. However, Jevons was not a very active member of the Unitarian church, and he seems to distance himself from Unitarianism in a letter to Gladstone:[57]

> I should like to add however that in venturing upon theological subjects I have been very much embarrassed to know how to express in a sufficiently strong and clear manner my own positive convictions on the subject without seeming to imply more than I mean. The fact is that I am by descent a Unitarian and as regards my own convictions am not perfectly clear.
>
> (Black 1977b: 36)

Jevons' rationalistic attitude towards religion increased with his age: when he was 15, he studied the Gospels and, during his stay in Australia, he expressed theological opinions, in his correspondence with Henrietta, that are very similar to the ideas expressed in Channing's lecture. In his statements about religion of the 1870s, he expresses critical opinions that seem to be more distanced from Unitarianism than before. But Jevons does not want to be called an atheist, which is implied in his statement that the Catholicism he hates so much is still better than irreligion and in his condemnation of Comte's positivism (in *The Principles of Science*; see below). Moreover, this evolution towards a more critical attitude is not very remarkable, as many Unitarians became more critical towards external authority (e.g. see the development of Martineau's thought). Even more important is the fact that Jevons was a scientist and not a theologian, and that he did not develop a complete theology. But he nevertheless tried to reconcile religion and science. Already in 1857, Jevons makes clear that his religious beliefs, although consistent with the teachings of science, are not derived from material nature. The world is, although stupendous, merely an inanimate and orderly machine without conceptions of good and evil. In 1857, Jevons writes, in a letter to Henrietta:

> For some six or seven years past I have been chiefly engaged in learning science and taking the very evident views of things, and the consequence has been to show me greatness and wonderful order or design in nature, but no feeling or actual good; on the contrary, we find evil or pain prevailing everywhere almost equally with pleasure. It is in the human mind (made as we know after the image of God), but particularly in the feelings of love and friendship that I can find any indications of positive good. Evil is inseparable from nature, and no writer has ever explained satisfactorily why evil should exist at all.
>
> (Black 1973: 288)

Religion and science: the role of evolution

The growing critical attitude of Unitarianism is accompanied by the rise of evolutionary theory, which generated interaction between American and British Unitarianism. Darwinism, of course, proved detrimental to biblical literalism, implying, as it did, that humanity was not a special divine creation at a specific point in past time, but rather the result of a long and often wasteful process whereby only the fittest species survived. The geological discoveries of Charles Lyell (1797–1875) – himself a Unitarian – suggested that the Earth's history was considerably longer than the Bible implied (the traditional date of Creation being 4004 BCE). Although popularly associated with Charles Darwin, evolutionism, of course, was a wider theory, which found its original expression in social theories such as those of Auguste Comte, Herbert Spencer and a wide variety of other thinkers who championed human progress. Of particular importance to our present discussion is the American Unitarian scholar James Freeman Clarke (1810–1888), best known for his highly influential and innovative two-volume work *Ten Great Religions: An Essay in Comparative Theology* (1871). Clarke's evolutionism finds expression in two areas: first, in the sphere of 'comparative religion' (as the study of world religions was then called) and, second, in his concept of Unitarianism. Clarke's *Ten Great Religions* treated the world's best known religious traditions thematically, comparing their ideas on broad areas such as God, the soul and the after-life. Despite his attempts to treat these various religions objectively, Clarke nonetheless argued that Christianity remained supreme: Hinduism had its caste system, Buddhism lacked a personal deity, and Islam taught predestination; thus, these religions, together with the other 'non-Christian' faiths, were to be viewed as stages on a journey, which paved the way for a new absolute faith that would be based on Christianity, but would transcend them all. This faith, of course, was Unitarianism.

Clarke's Unitarianism, the emergent final religion, was defined in five main points:

> The Fatherhood of God
> The Brotherhood of Man
> The Leadership of Jesus
> Salvation by Character
> The Continuity of Human Development [. . .] or the Progress of Mankind, onward and upward for ever.
>
> (quoted in Chryssides 1998: 77)

The first four points are reminiscent of the Unitarianism of Channing and others, but the final point is simultaneously an acknowledgement of evolutionism and a vote of confidence in humanity's presumed ability to progress. Although these ideas flourished initially in America, Clarke's book was well known on both sides of the Atlantic, and it is not uncommon to find older Unitarian church premises in Britain on which Clarke's five principles are displayed.

Herbert Spencer's version of evolutionary theory was especially influential in the United States, although in England, Darwin was opposed to Spencer's synthesis, arguing that it was not of any use to him; he even disliked Spencer's personality (Moore 1979: 161–6). This is not surprising, as Spencer maintained the Lamarckian principle of the inheritance of acquired characteristics. He regarded natural selection, as such, as an inadequate explanation for evolution (which is not exceptional in a pre-genetic age), but he also needed Lamarckism to maintain the similarity between biological and socio-cultural evolution (Peel 1971: 142–3). Spencer's obsession with creating a complete synthesis attracted much criticism, but it also allowed reconciliation of religion and science.

In the first part of his *First Principles*, Spencer (1898: 3–24) argues that there must exist a harmonious relation between religion and science. All beliefs contain at least some core of truth, and the probability of truthfulness increases when more people share the same beliefs. The idea would be to find out which thoughts are shared in conflicting beliefs (such as religion and science) to arrive at statements that are beyond doubt. Spencer sees science as a higher development of common knowledge that emerged out of an evolutionary process. The body of science consists of accumulated modifications due to the intercourse of the human mind with changing environmental conditions. Religion cannot therefore simply be dismissed, as it resulted through criticism and reflection of countless generations in 2000 years. However, the element common to all religions and to science must necessarily be a highly abstract proposition:

> Neither such dogmas as those of the Trinitarian and Unitarian, nor any such idea as that of propitiation, common though it may be to all religions, can serve as the desired basis of agreement; for Science cannot recognize beliefs like these: they lie beyond its sphere.
>
> (Spencer 1898: 23)

From the scientific point of view, the relevant propositions must be underlying all the scientific subdisciplines, and not be particular to one of them (Spencer 1898: 23–4). Spencer (1898: 41–6) then continues arguing that all fundamental conceptions of rational theology are necessarily self-destructive and that none of them is logically defensible. But all religious beliefs – and even atheism – have in common that there is something to be explained and that 'such and such is the explanation'. The existence of the world as such and all its elements and surroundings is the mystery that is in need of explanation and interpretation. The fact that 'the Power which the Universe manifests to us is utterly inscrutable' is the basis of reconciliation of all facts. Mysticism is therefore reconciling different religious beliefs and science.[58] Ultimate scientific ideas, such as time and space, are also representations of realities that cannot be fully comprehended. They are just symbols of the actual, and human knowledge is incapable of absolute knowledge (Spencer 1898: 66–8). This quotation is particularly illuminating:

> Common sense asserts the existence of a reality; Objective Science proves

that this reality cannot be what we think it; Subjective Science shows why we cannot think of it as it is, and yet are compelled to think of it as existing; and in this assertion of a Reality utterly inscrutable in nature, Religion finds an assertion essentially coinciding with her own.

(Spencer 1898: 99)

The present state of thought about the world is the evolutionary outcome of successive civilizations. In due course, the conflict between science and religion will diminish: science has to become fully convinced that all its explanations are merely approximations and that absolute knowledge can never be reached, whereas religion has to become fully convinced that the mystery it contemplates is absolute (Spencer 1898: 107). Before such reconciliation can be achieved, a long evolutionary process is required. All forms of thought, of science and religion, must be in accordance with the people that develop these forms. Aboriginals represent divine agencies in concrete and ordinary forms; polytheism is idealizing different personalities; and monotheism is even more abstract. The recognition of highly abstract mystical ideas is a final step in the reconciliation of religion and science (Spencer 1898: 44–5, 119).

In *The Data of Ethics* (1879), Spencer discusses the evolution of conduct. Higher phases of evolution are reached when acts are ever more adjusted to ends. Good conduct is relatively more evolved and furthers self-preservation, whereas bad conduct is relatively less evolved and directed towards self-destruction (Spencer 1879: 25). The value of self-preservation or self-destruction depends, however, on the optimistic or pessimistic attitude of the agent. Good conduct is then seen as promoting pleasure and happiness, whereas bad conduct leads to pain and misery (Spencer 1879: 26–30). Spencer then refutes other ethical theories because they do not recognize that their conceptions (perfection, virtue and intuition) rely on notions of pleasures and pains. It is then somewhat surprising that Spencer also criticizes utilitarianism, as this branch of ethics also takes the 'natural causation' towards pleasures and pains into account. Spencer argues, however, that utilitarians determine utility only by observation of results, whereas he wants to arrive at it in a deductive way by reasoning from general principles (Spencer 1879: 56–8). Spencer wants to replace 'empirical utilitarianism' with 'rational utilitarianism', which deduces general principles 'from the processes of life as carried on under established conditions of existence' (Spencer 1879: 61).[59]

Ethical evolution, then, consists of change in motives, and even the complete disappearance of all motives as soon as a high state of moral consciousness has been reached. Persistence in performing a duty ends up in pleasurable activities and the obligation disappears. For instance, the activities of a businessman or the fostering of children by parents can be directly gratified by these actions themselves, without the interference of some sense of obligation. Spencer concludes that, in a high state of civilization, all compulsions from without will practically disappear (Spencer 1879: 127–31).[60] The evolution of social groups goes hand in hand with a larger division of labour, which necessitates overcoming the antagonism between individual and social welfare. At first, co-operation is seen as compulsory, and conflicts are omnipresent, but the gradual diminution of war is accompanied by the tendency for compulsory co-operation to make room for voluntary co-operation (Spencer 1898: 148–9).

The concept of 'race' is a major problem in Spencer's thought. Fieser (1993) argues that Spencer lacks a clearly defined evolutionary spectrum of social behaviour. This prevents him from using objective criteria to distinguish highly evolved from less evolved behavioural interaction in different cultures and societies. Spencer's discussion of races should be placed within the framework of his Lamarckian approach. He was unable to reconcile or choose between the environmentalist and hereditarian traditions, and his discussions about race are rather confusing. This resulted in:

> [. . .] an elastic doctrine, which permitted what Stocking calls a 'bland and blind shuttling' between race and environment, and was both ideologically useful and scientifically unhelpful. Without abandoning any theory Spencer shifted from the radical optimism of his early writings, where he shows himself convinced of the variability of human nature and sceptical of the fixity of species, [. . .] to a pessimism and practical conservatism which played down the present action of the environment in favour of the sum of past environmental influence, 'organized' as character or race.
>
> (Peel 1971: 143–6)

Spencer's views on slavery are somewhat clearer. Regarding individual liberty as the apex of human evolution, Spencer's essay *The Man versus the State* (1844) argues forcefully against undue state interference with the individual, comparing this to slavery, which he regards unequivocally as reprehensible.

Although Spencer does not feature explicitly in much Unitarian writing of the period, Ralph Waldo Emerson met him during the latter's visit to England from 1832 to 1834, and the American Unitarian minister writer Francis Ellingwood Abbot (1836–1903) drew substantially on Spencer's work, although he regarded Spencer's evolutionary theory as unduly 'mechanistic', proposing a 'vitalist' form of evolution, whereby progress and change came from within, rather than without, living ('vital') phenomena. James Martineau devotes a brief discussion to Spencer in his *The Seat of Authority of Religion*, arguing that, while Spencer may have demonstrated the means whereby living beings develop through time, this bears no ethical implications regarding what one *ought* to do about human evolution and change.

Whatever the conceptual connections between slavery, liberty, evolution and morality, Unitarians tended to be divided on the issue of slavery. William Lloyd Garrison (1805–1879) founded the Anti-Slavery Society in America, and Channing's *Slavery* (1835) described the practice as 'barbarism'. Theodore Parker, however, deserves the greatest recognition for his anti-slavery campaigning, being the author of many anti-slavery tracts and actively helping fugitive slaves to escape from their owner. The American Unitarian Universalist General Assembly passed a resolution in 1843 opposing slavery. However, it would be wrong to suppose that Unitarians were unequivocally abolitionist: particularly in the cotton-growing areas of America, vested interests caused many Unitarian slave owners to support the status quo.

Similarly diverse attitudes were also to be found in Britain. Robert Hibbert, the founder of the Hibbert Trust, reportedly owned 400 slaves in Jamaica, and other Unitarians had black servants: although they were not called slaves, their working and living conditions were poor. The Unitarian minister, John Yates, caused deep offence by preaching against slavery to his Liverpool congregation in 1788, although Joseph Priestley gained more support among his Birmingham congregation after preaching on the subject in the same year. Nineteenth-century Unitarians who opposed slavery included Josiah Wedgwood, Lant Carpenter and Jevons' grandfather, William Roscoe, who lost his seat after supporting anti-slavery legislation in parliament.

Jevons was particularly favourable towards Spencer's evolutionary ethics, which strengthened his initial belief that science and religion are not incompatible, but complementary. In a letter to John Mills dated 18 November 1873, Jevons reports that he read Spencer's *First Principles*, published for the first time in 1862. It is not possible to find out the exact date when Jevons read the book, but the letter suggests that he must have read it several years before 1873.[61] Jevons does not hesitate to embrace the 'truth' of Spencer's evolutionary principles, although he complains that Spencer tried to develop a large system that would cover every aspect of knowledge (physics, biology, psychology, sociology), which makes it vulnerable to criticism.[62] Jevons argues that evolutionary theory is especially fruitful when applied to ethics and, in 1879, he refers to *The Data of Ethics* that appeared in the same year (Jevons 1879a: 536).

> Evolution is a striving ever towards the better and the happier. [. . .] Let mankind be thrown back a hundred times, and a hundred times the better tendencies of evolution will re-assert themselves. [. . .] Retrogression may result as well as progression. But I apprehend that retrogression can only occur where the environment of a living species is altered to its detriment. [. . .] According to Spencer, as I venture to interpret his theory, we are the latest manifestation of an all-prevailing tendency toward the good – the happy. Creation is not yet concluded, and there is no one of us who may not become conscious in his heart that he is no Automaton, no mere lump of Protoplasm, but the Creature of a Creator.
>
> (Jevons 1879a: 538)

These quotations illustrate the remarkable role that Spencer's evolutionary thought plays in Jevons' thinking. The evolutionary perspective lets Jevons integrate his religious beliefs in a view on the world as growing towards higher moral consciousness and rationality. Like Spencer, Jevons argues that there is no conflict at all between science and religion. On the contrary, they are both directed towards truth and, therefore, they cannot contradict each other. Jevons congratulated John Herschel for his condemnation of the Theological Declaration of Scientific Man, which equated freedom of enquiry with a tendency to irreligion (Black 1977c: 60). Jevons even intended to write the Tenth Bridgewater Treatise (following Charles Babbage's Ninth Bridgewater Treatise) to show the perfect compatibility between science and religion, but he never completed this work (H. A. Jevons 1886: 451).

In *The Principles of Science*, Jevons devotes a section on the theory of evolution,[63] followed by a section on the possibility of divine interference (Jevons 1874: 761–9). Jevons embraces Spencer's idea that the homogeneous is unstable and differentiates itself in the process of evolutionary development. A variety of human institutions and characters emerged. He recognizes that evolutionary theory has not been proved, but nevertheless he adheres to its truthfulness. It is certainly not in conflict with theology, as it does not lead to the conclusion that creation was and is impossible. Evolutionary theory discloses several natural laws that explain how primitive life evolved to humankind by processes of adaptation to changing circumstances – but the initial distribution of atoms in the primeval world is very important as well. Jevons argues that this initial distribution is the result of the 'arbitrary choice of the Creator', which could have been very different and, therefore, present life would have been very different as well. Evolutionary theory tells us only that similar circumstances will lead to similar results because the same laws apply, but this is not in conflict with an initial act of creation. In close accordance with Spencer's *First Principles*, Jevons states that it would be absurd to deny that anything exists, and that it might therefore be equally conceivable that the world was created out of nothing or that it existed from eternity. He also states clearly that science cannot disprove the possibility of divine intervention, which implies that a positivist attitude does not necessarily lead to materialism or atheism. God may disclose new agents or sources of energy, or he may annihilate or create additional portions of material nature.[64] Jevons also maintains his distance from Comte's positivistic philosophy, by arguing – like Spencer – that scientific reflection on higher notions of creation must necessarily end up in contradictions.

It cannot be considered merely a coincidence that Jevons devotes, at the end of his life and especially since the late 1870s (after his reading of Spencer), much more time to societal problems that have strong ethical and social dimensions.[65] Almost all his publications prior to 1867 are concerned with 'hard' economic and scientific questions (railways, business cycles, coal, money, meteorology, etc.) with only a few notable exceptions (such as Jevons 1858). His interest in social questions, especially trade unions and industrial partnerships, increases after 1867, probably after his reading of Spencer's *First Principles*. After the publication of the fourth part of his criticism of Mill (Jevons 1879b), which contains a section on Spencer's *Data of Ethics*, several writings on social and ethical questions emerge: experimental legislation and the drink traffic (1880), free public libraries (1881), married women in factories (1882), *The State in Relation to Labour* (1882) and museums (1881–82).[66]

Religion and science in Jevons' economics

Black (1995a: 190, 195) argues that there occurred a transition in Jevons' thought towards increased interventionism. Black recognizes that, after 1867, Jevons' 'increasing faith in the validity of Spencer's theory of evolution was combined with decreasing faith in the validity of laissez-faire as a guide for economic policy'. In the second section of this chapter, we argued that Unitarians struggled with the 'contradiction' between the need for individual self-improvement, on the one hand, and active interventionism, on the other hand. This 'contradiction' can also be depicted as a tension existing between a belief in scientific principles on the one hand – the laws of economics – and the recognition that moral and intellectual self-improvement is impossible as long as the first necessaries of life are still out of reach. Unitarians concluded that a rational mode of living had to be imposed on the poor before they could benefit from education. Jevons tried to resolve this paradox by restricting the scientific analysis to what can be accounted for in terms of the accumulation of wealth, and by suggesting that a 'higher' calculus of pleasures and pains is needed when 'higher' motives interfere. Interventionism could then be justified by pointing out those 'higher' motives. The scientific basis of Jevons' economics is utilitarianism and the mechanics of utility and self-interest; like many Unitarians, this scientific belief is combined with an emphasis on active interventionism directed towards more possibilities for self-improvement, and evolutionary theory not only shows that there *should* be development towards the 'good' and the 'happy', but also that there *will* be such a development (at least in Jevons' interpretation). We should also take into account that, originally, Jevons' approach towards economics was embedded in a larger 'science of man' project.

The 'science of man' includes both religion and political economy. Although Jevons' economics is part of this larger 'science of man project', we should emphasize that he pleads for subdivision. The abstract theory must be distinguished from the empirical part, from applied theory and from the arts of finance and administration (Jevons 1911: xvii). The same applies to the moral sciences in general: its different branches (political economy, moral philosophy, jurisprudence, political philosophy, hygienic science, penal jurisprudence and 'a vast body of Statistical, or Social science') should be differentiated from each other (Black 1977a: 8). This is Jevons' most explicit definition of moral philosophy: 'Moral philosophy considers the grounds of men's duties and obligations towards each other, and the effects of their characters and actions on the general good' (Black 1981: 55). Economics, or political economy, is much more restricted in scope: it discusses the source of the welfare of nations, which is wealth (Black 1977a: 6). Abstract economic theory is clearly differentiated from moral philosophy or ethics:

> It is the lowest ranks of feelings which we here treat. The calculus of utility aims at supplying the ordinary wants of man at the least cost of labour. Each labourer, in the absence of other motives, is supposed to devote his energy to the accumulation of wealth. A higher calculus of moral right and wrong

would be needed to show how he may best employ that wealth for the good of others as well as himself.

(Jevons 1911: 27)

This is compatible with Jevons' general views on science, religion and ethics that we encountered above. Material nature does not contain goodness; it can only be found in the human mind. Nature is depicted as a mechanical machine and should be studied by the natural sciences. Abstract economic theory is the mechanical analogy of these natural sciences: it is restricted to an investigation of the social world as a mechanical machine, and no ethical or religious considerations are taken into account. Jevons refutes the claims of some 'sentimental writers' who regard economics as a 'dismal science', because its scope is restricted to wealth. These authors depict economics as a mechanical and miserable body of theories, whereas they hold true that a moral science should be concerned with sympathies, feelings and duties. Jevons uses an analogy from the natural sciences to refute this opinion: division of labour implies that some people investigate the mechanical aspects of iron, while other researchers devote their time to the study of its electrical or magnetic aspects. A physician may conclude that the health of a particular person will be fostered if he goes to the sea, but this person may decide otherwise by taking other considerations into account. This is the position of economics: charity for humanitarian reasons remains possible, but abstract economic theory teaches that this may endanger the future accumulation of wealth (Black 1977a: 7–8). It is, however, remarkable that all the policy measures that Jevons lists in his *Primer* have actually been undertaken by middle-class reformers holding Unitarian beliefs: establishment of institutions that further public education and provision of means to enable the poor to undertake actions directed towards self-improvement.

There is absolutely nothing in the science [of political economy] to dissuade the rich man from spending his wealth generously and yet wisely. He may prudently help his relatives and friends, he may establish useful public institutions, such as free public libraries, museums, public parks, dispensaries, etc., he may assist in educating the poor or promoting institutions for higher education; he may relieve any who are suffering from misfortunes which could not have been provided against, cripples, blind people, and all who are absolutely disabled from helping themselves, are proper objects of the rich man's charity.

(Jevons 1878: 9–10)

Sandra Peart (1990) demonstrates that Jevons refers to Benthamite principles for his economic policy on several occasions.[67] He does not use a theory of 'abstract rights', but evaluates policy measures according to the principle of 'the greatest good of the greatest number'. A legislator should take general principles of different disciplines into account (ethics, economics, jurisprudence, etc.), but should also not neglect public opinion. The pretension to create wide-ranging social reforms should be abandoned, and attention should instead be devoted to incremental reforms, using practical wisdom on a case-by-case base.[68] Different degrees of 'happiness' should be balanced against each other, and prices may be used to measure utility in policy matters. However, Peart (1990a: 287–8) identifies two problems in Jevons' approach. First of all, it is not clear how Jevons would rank 'objectively' different policy measures. 'Intellectual' pleasures receive a high priority, some people's happiness receives a higher weight, and measures that ameliorate working class conditions are favoured. Moreover, Jevons does not specify a mechanism that would enable an estimation of consumers' pleasures when prices are unavailable. Peart argues that Jevons' application of utilitarianism to economic policy contains some implicit value judgements 'concerning the general development of society and the amelioration of working class conditions', but she does not investigate the origin of these subjective judgements. White (1994b) remarks that Jevons' theory should not be investigated within the framework of the positive/normative dichotomy and that the concept of 'value judgements' does not make sense. Bowman (1997b: 200) argues that 'Jevons' advocacy of an expansion of public works was grounded in his utility theory of value'.

Both White and Bowman thus emphasize the importance of the 'hierarchy of motives' argument, but it remains unclear how Jevons justifies and uses this 'hierarchy'. Our reading of Jevons' work suggests that this 'hierarchy' is derived from his Unitarian beliefs and his interpretation of Spencer. The Unitarian quest for moral self-improvement through the use of reason is hidden behind seemingly utilitarian policy prescriptions. A free library is better than a racecourse because the library allows moral improvement through education. Jevons' economic policy proposals contain many examples that seem to be inspired by the type of middle-class ideology that is especially to be found among Unitarians. 'Hard scientific facts', for instance regarding the behaviour of rational economic agents, are complemented with pleas for active interventionism that should enable the poor to undertake actions directed towards self-improvement.

In the previous chapter, we discussed Jevons' use of 'representative individuals' and the notion of 'character', where the Victorian middle class is used as a yardstick for evaluation. Earlier in this chapter, we mentioned that Unitarians believe that the formation of an improved character is essential, because otherwise no religious warmth can emerge. It is unclear to what extent improvement of people with presumed inferior character (due to class, race or gender) can be achieved. In Jevons, we encounter a mixture of enlightened belief in education and prejudiced opinions against certain parts of the population, which is certainly not unusual in the nineteenth century. Nevertheless, Jevons does believe that policies to ameliorate working-class conditions and attitudes are possible, desirable and required. His policy prescriptions for moral and social improvement are in perfect accordance with (his) Unitarian beliefs and with his initial 'science of man' project.

His work on economic subjects contains many examples of this economic policy. Already in 1858, Jevons argues that the character of a city is connected with the character of its inhabitants, and he describes the 'Rocks' as a dirty and unhealthy part of Sydney that is inhabited by immoral and drunken people. The absence of sanitation should be condemned, as proper sanitation may foster the elevation of the morality of the masses (Jevons 1858). In the next chapter, we review Jevons' policy proposal for public performances of music. Public libraries should receive sufficient funding, because they would give rise to increased morality and thus to a reduction in poor rates and less expenditure on crime.[69] Jevons does not condemn reading literature as a distracter from practical subjects, because the alternative would be even worse: reading of vulgar works or no reading at all. Public libraries therefore increase education and general intelligence (Jevons 1883: 32–48). Jevons' oeuvre contains many similar policy prescriptions regarding the elevation of the 'character' of the masses.

Jevons' *Experimental Legislation and the Drink Traffic*, published in the *Contemporary Review* in 1880 and republished in *Methods of Social Reform* (1883), may serve as an example. The main goal of this particular social policy is the diminution of public drunkenness and a change in the attitudes and behaviour of lower class people. The Scandinavian working class seems to serve as an example, as Jevons mentions the 'orderly polished lower-class population of Sweden'. However, Jevons recognizes that policy measures cannot be universal, as local circumstances must be taken into account. 'Even between English towns the differences of magnitude, race, occupation, and local government are often so great that it is by no means certain that the same scheme will succeed equally in all' (Jevons 1883: 268). A difference in habits must therefore be taken into account, experiments must be conducted, and sufficient statistical data must be collected in order to measure policy effectiveness. This 'change-of-attitude-policy' can be applied to many cases:

> *Earth-hunger* is a very potent passion, and I believe it is that from which the Irish people are really suffering. Bread and bacon are not the only good things an Irish peasant might aspire to; a place to call his own, a share of the air and sunlight in his native isle, and a land-bank in which to save up the strokes of his pick and spade, might work moral wonders.
>
> (Jevons 1884: 274)

An improvement in character is therefore required, and the middle class (and the Swedish working class) is used as a yardstick. The 'experimental' approach implies that only experience can show whether it is possible to alter particular 'characters' by specific policies. We may expect that some policies are successful and others not, and that some characters can be changed (in certain ways) whereas others cannot. As experience can be our only guide, this may explain why there are no general statements about the possibility of altering 'characters' in general in Jevons' work.

Conclusion

In this chapter, we have tried to shed a different light on William Stanley Jevons. Unitarian by descent, his religious thoughts grow and mature in a context in which Unitarianism itself changes thoroughly and develops a stronger critical attitude. Jevons defends the unity of science and religion, and combines abstract and mechanical economic theory with economic and social policy proposals that are specifically directed towards improvement of 'character'. Evolutionist thought reinforces the need for this interventionist policy, as it not only shows that there should be, but also that there will be, development towards the good (according to Jevons). This chapter does not claim that the development of Jevons' religious thought must be a part of any assessment of his economics, nor that Jevons developed some 'religious economic thought'. It is also quite conceivable that different economists, although coming from different backgrounds, end up with similar ideas.

7 Jevons and music

Aping the upper class[70]

(with Ernest Mathijs, University of Wales at Aberystwyth, UK)

Introduction[71]

This chapter investigates an unpublished manuscript on music by William Stanley Jevons. In the first section, we analyse the origin of the manuscript, and show that it should be seen as a part of Jevons' utilitarian 'science of man' project. The manuscript also serves as a justification for the time Jevons devotes to playing music, and it was meant as an improvement to the already existing literature on the subject. In the second section, we summarize the chapter 'On the Functions of Music', and highlight several aspects. Music is partly an object of enjoyment, but it fulfils educational and moralizing purposes as well. An 'intellectual cleavage' in Jevons' ideas on music appears, when he argues that lower forms of music may be enjoyed by everyone, but that higher forms require education and training. His diagrams on the classification of the arts reflect this 'cleavage'. In the third section, we investigate the aesthetic context of Jevons' manuscript, and argue that it belongs to the Anglo-Saxon aesthetic tradition of Shaftesbury. Although Jevons remains within this tradition, his general disinterest in aesthetic categories (the beautiful and the sublime) is explained by his utilitarian approach. The 'use' of art (in a utilitarian sense) is Jevons' concern, and not the metaphysics of the beautiful. This becomes clear in the fourth section, in which we investigate Jevons' policy prescriptions regarding public performances of music. These cheap and easily accessible means of spreading culture may operate as tools to elevate moral consciousness among the people. We argue that Jevons' solitary and intellectual conception of music may be ill-suited for this purpose.

The origin of Jevons' music manuscript

In order to understand the meaning of Jevons' music manuscript, we have to investigate the context in which it was written. The manuscript is one of the numerous products of Jevons' lonely hours in Australia. Jevons arrived in Sydney in October 1854, where he started his position as an assayer at the Australian Mint. His acceptance of this position was partly motivated by the narrow financial situation at home, after the bankruptcy of his father following the 'railway boom crisis' of 1847–8. On 5 January 1855, Jevons writes in his journal that he does not intend to stay in Australia and remain an assayer for the rest of his life. On the contrary, he looks forward to returning to England after having collected a small sum of money. He would like to start over again at home, but now with some capital and with several years of 'colonial experience' (Black and Könekamp 1972: 110). Jevons fills his spare time with various scientific investigations (meteorology, botanics, geology), excursions and music.

In February 1856, Jevons receives the news of the sudden death of his father, Thomas Jevons. In Chapter 2, we argue that this sad news enters Jevons' reflections on subjects regarding 'selfishness'. He has always been somewhat preoccupied with this subject, but the death of his father brings in a stronger personal dimension.[72] Jevons would be pleased if he knew that he had pleased his father, and he wonders whether this reasoning is induced by feelings of love towards his father, or simply by selfish feelings. He concludes that 'all our thoughts and motives [. . .] never seem to spring from a perfectly pure source' (Black 1973: 212). Moreover, his father's death leads Jevons to a general questioning of what ought to be achieved in life. The outcome of his reflection is a utilitarian framework in which a 'science of man' emerges. We argue that the music manuscript is part of this 'science'. Jevons' personal worries are mixed up with his scientific investigations, and he seems to derive the basic principles of this framework from what he had learned from his father.[73] Thomas Jevons always defended the idea that a person should 'be *good* and *honourable*' and should 'strive to make himself of *use & value* in the world' (Black 1973: 214). Jevons' reflections on selfishness and usefulness are expressed in a letter to his sister Henrietta:

> I have enough ado indeed to find out what I am myself exactly and to persuade myself that it is what is right, and to this end I have often entered into sorts of long mental discussions as to what the word (of all the most disagreeable) '*selfish*' really means. Generally, however, they terminate much about where they began, and I have lately begun to accept the wish to be *unselfish* as tantamount to the fact.
>
> (Black 1973: 240–1)

Jevons states that human behaviour should be judged by an investigation of motives. These motives should be guided by 'principles' of truthfulness and honesty of purpose, with a real regard for the sake of others and for oneself. This procedure may be too 'indefinite and uninviting' for most minds, but Jevons does not see other options. Jevons would like to be as unselfish as possible, but he is not at all convinced that similar processes of mind go on in other persons. As words are insufficient to prove the purity of purposes, acts may be the only way to show one's honesty (Black 1973: 241–2).[74] Jevons uses this utilitarian framework to judge his own daily activities and, here, he arrives at some trouble. He is always occupied with intellectual activities, and he even complains that he does not have enough time to undertake everything he would like to (Black 1973: 225). He is very worried about how to allocate his scarce time to his various occupations, because he would like to maximize his use and value for the world. On the other hand, Jevons does not give the impression of being concerned with others. He reports to Henrietta that he had visitors, but could not spend more than twenty minutes with them because he was buried in a particular subject. He wonders whether his sisters will tolerate his 'abstract attitude' once he returns to England (JA10/1/37a). He writes to Henrietta:

> Sometimes I begin to feel more like a misanthropist than is comfortable although in theory I profess the very opposite. I am not very amiable or well fitted to please small tea-parties; it may be very well to amuse and please people in general but it scarcely seems my vocation. Cannot a division of labour be allowed so that those who are amiable may exercise their talents in small talk and good humour, while I betake myself to dreary work and thought? This is all that I ask and surely I offer people in general a very favourable bargain. It is a petty that they cannot see it as I see it.
>
> (JA10/1/40a)

Elsewhere, Jevons writes that it would be 'bad economy' to drop his current activities and to work solely for others, although it would certainly be an action induced by good motives. It may be more profitable in the long term to devote much time to reading and scientific study, although it may appear to be selfish at first sight (Black 1973: 276–7). Jevons would like to be 'powerfully good' not to just one or several persons, but towards a nation or even the world. He would therefore like to use the powers of his mind to maximize his usefulness for the world. He thinks that the most powerful ability of his mind lies in a strong disposition to classify things. He is not so good when it comes to forming new thoughts and opinions, but his strength consists of developing already existing ideas 'into something symmetrical' (Black 1973: 308). Although Jevons would like to be a practical man who sees the effects following the cause, he is more suited to becoming a student of remote and abstract causes and, in this sense, could be a 'great good to all succeeding generations' (Black 1973: 335).

The same utilitarian framework enables Jevons to justify his scientific investigations and his aversion towards small talk and tea-parties. On the other hand, he remains unsatisfied with other people considering him 'strangely unsociable and uncompromising' (Black 1973: 302). Jevons complains about not having a 'mind' to talk to: it would be absurd to express serious thoughts to persons who cannot respond to them or think them absurd (Black 1973: 311). Jevons prefers solitude, as this is a requisite in order to form 'earnest thoughts'; almost nothing can be learned from experiences with ordinary people (Black 1973: 337). Although Jevons may exaggerate his solitude,[75] it is clear that he prefers solitary scientific investigations over social gatherings. He does not sleep much, and spends a lot of his spare time on the 'science of man', a collection of scientific studies that are based on Jevons' utilitarian framework (see Chapter 3).

Just as in physics, the science of man is directed to the discovery of general principles and laws. The science rests on the suppositions that man is 'a phenomenon in which *effect* is always connected with *cause*', and that there have to be 'causes to make people good and bad, happy and miserable, rich and poor, as well as strong and feeble'. The science of man should take numerous data into account, because each human being possesses animal powers, a logical mind and a series of emotions, and is placed in circumstances that are continuously changing (Black 1973: 361–2). Jevons' project is therefore a heterogeneous collection of different disciplines, and he devotes much time to different surveys. One part of this large project concerns 'towns and cities', and is directed to the discovery of the 'nature' of particular cities. It would consist of analysing the constitution and causes of cities, the relative character of their parts and the relative character of particular cities (Black 1973: 327).[76] Another part is economics, 'a sort of vague mathematics which calculates the causes and effects of man's industry, and shows how it may best be applied' (Black 1973: 321). Jevons' music manuscript is another part of this 'science of man'. The chapter on 'Functions' opens with the observation that music is an 'integral part of man' (JA6/47/8). Moreover, Jevons' comparison of different art forms is couched in utilitarian terms (see below). A first motivation for Jevons to prepare the manuscript is therefore that it is a part of the 'science of man' project. We elaborate on this subject in the next section.

We have already stated above that Jevons' project is mixed up with personal worries. Besides being part of the 'science of man', the manuscript is therefore also an attempt to justify his love for music and the time he devotes to playing his harmonium. Jevons bought the harmonium in 1855 and considered it a 'first rate thing' to have an instrument in the 'Australian wilds' (Black 1973: 162). He purchased several pieces of music and practised a lot. He reports his progress and his judgement of the pieces to his sister Henrietta, who is very fond of music as well. She is in fact the only person Jevons communicates with on musical topics. Jevons states that he does not play to please other people, but he would like to understand the music in his own way. He compares this with reading a book, which is also an activity never to be performed to please others (Black 1973: 225). Although Jevons' solitude may be exaggerated when it comes to his scientific work, it may be a proper characterization of his attitude towards music. We argue later that Jevons' solitary conception of music has severe consequences for his policy recommendations. Jevons spends a lot of time playing the harmonium. On 25 November 1856, he writes that 'music proceeds well and I shall know half the music in the world in a few years if I play as much as I do know' (JA10/1/27). Music is very important for Jevons:

> Music is always to me the same, a condition of my existence, a part of me. I believe I could live a *life of Music*. If our physical nature did not interfere, I can almost conceive it possible that a man might play music *ad infinitum* and still never tire. [. . .] Now I think that nothing less than a life time would quite satisfy my musical thirst while I find with concern that a single hour per day out of the 24, considerably interferes with other affairs equally or more important. Music thus ought to be a rare but still a legitimate and occasional delight.
>
> (Black 1973: 319–20)

This quotation suggests that the music manuscript should also be seen as an attempt to justify the time Jevons devotes to playing music, as it interferes with other activities. A third motivation for writing the manuscript is Jevons' general dissatisfaction with the already existing literature on the subject. On 3 May 1856, he reports reading Spencer's *A Rudimentary and Practical Treatise on Music* (1850), which he considers '*excessively dull* as well as rather difficult' (Black 1973: 227). On 3 July 1856, he writes to Henrietta:

> I enclose you a long affair which I have been writing lately. Wishing to read and understand a little of the principles of music, and being rather disgusted with the superficial uninteresting sort of books I can find on it, I thought I would write a book of my own which however imperfect would indeed teach me more than any body else's. [. . .] Voici Chapters 1 and 2. As it must be so very short, I do not know whether I make it very plain, if not get other books to help you out, for instance Spencer's *Rudimentary Treatise on Music.*
>
> (JA10/1/25)

Black and Könekamp argued that Jevons' music manuscript contained a new system of notation, and that it has not survived (Black and Könekamp 1972: 32; Black 1973: 243). However, there is no evidence that the book was on musical notation. Jevons does indeed writes in a letter that the current system of notation is 'stupidly contrived', but he adds that 'I should improve it if I think I had much to do with it' (Black 1973: 227). It seems clear that the manuscript contains a general survey of music theory instead, as it was intended as an improvement to the already existing literature on the subject. Moreover, the Henrietta section of the John Rylands Library in Manchester contains a document (JA10/1/32b) that is certainly part of the larger manuscript to be found in the same archive (JA6/47/8). As Jevons sent the manuscript to Henrietta, this is good evidence that the manuscript under consideration is the one mentioned in Jevons' letters.[77] Jevons reports sending a new chapter of the book on 1 October 1856 (Black 1973: 243) and another chapter ('a longer one than ever') on 25 November 1856 (JA10/1/27). On 4 April 1857, Jevons states that he does not have time to continue the book, nor does he have something in his head to write about.

We therefore conclude that the 'missing manuscript' is archived at the John Rylands Library, and that it was written in the last quarter of 1856 and the first quarter of 1857. It should be seen as part of the larger 'science of man' project, as a justification of Jevons' love for music and as his attempt to improve the already existing literature on the subject. In the next section, we investigate this manuscript in detail.

Jevons' music manuscript

The manuscript *On the Science and Art of Music* is located at the John Rylands Library with reference JA6/47/1–17, and it consists of fifty pages. Most of the chapters deal with physical and technical aspects of music: The Nature of Sound & the Undulatory Theory (chap. I); On the Harmony of Sounds (chap. II); On the

Complete or Chromatic Scale and the Adjustment of Notes or Temperament (chap. III); On Melody (chap. IV); On the Functions of Music; On Musical Rhythm and Time; and some preparatory writings.[78] We focus on the chapter 'On the Functions of Music', as it contains Jevons' most explicit aesthetic ideas. We give first a general overview of the content of this chapter and, thereafter, we examine several aspects in detail: the essential character of music, its intellectual aspects and Jevons' concept of 'perceptive pleasure'. We then examine and compare three different diagrams to be found at different places in the archive (JA6/45/4, JA6/45/5, JA10/1/32b). To clarify our arguments, we add material from the correspondence between Jevons and Henrietta (JA10; Black 1973). The appendix to this chapter contains a complete transcription of the 'Functions' chapter (JA6/47/8) as well as the most elaborate diagram (JA6/45/4; Figure 1).

In the first paragraph of the 'Functions' chapter, Jevons states that the 'functions' of music should not be reduced to its 'use', as music is more than a simple instrument of pleasure. It is an integral part of every individual, although the importance attached to music is not equal for every person. When the 'sense' for music is once developed, it becomes an indissoluble part of the person (like the other senses). Jevons would like to investigate the precise place that music occupies 'among the occupations and capacities of men'. Music is essential because its experience gives rise to essential feelings. Everybody knows these feelings 'to a greater or less degree': they result from the contemplation of 'subjects of interest, beauty or sublimity'. These feelings remove the mind from its ordinary affairs and thoughts, but do not lead to conclusions or future purposes. The hearer receives 'a sort of confident moral strength', which is not lasting, as it disappears as soon as the music is over and the daily duties and sorrows appear again. Jevons lists other means of achieving these feelings: a walk in the countryside, sight-seeing, observation of architectural or engineering works, or listening to poetry. The feelings arise from the contemplation of anything that possesses 'a degree of fresh interest, beauty or grandeur'. Jevons is unable to investigate the cause of these feelings, but it is clear that they do not depend on knowledge. No scientific knowledge of the subjects of 'interest, beauty or grandeur' is required: the beauty of a forest does not increase if the perceiver gains botanical acquaintance, and the enjoyment of music does not presuppose knowledge of harmonical composition. These feelings belong to the perception and not to the reason, and they are inexplicable. These feelings are similar to the feebler feelings that are produced by the contemplation of 'beautiful' scientific facts or knowledge, or of 'fixed principles and enduring convictions and emotions which form religion and all our sense of love and duty'. This fact notwithstanding, Jevons considers the former feelings to be 'far below the level' of the latter feelings. He then defines the concept of 'perceptive pleasure' as the emotions 'produced by subjects of nature or art, through the medium of the senses or mind, but without the necessary exercise of the higher faculties of reason'. These emotions can arise from different sources, and Jevons classifies them by the 'sense or means through which they act on the mind': the sense of hearing, the sense of sight, and 'poetical ideas or mental pictures of beauty' that arise through the medium of the mind itself. Only a small

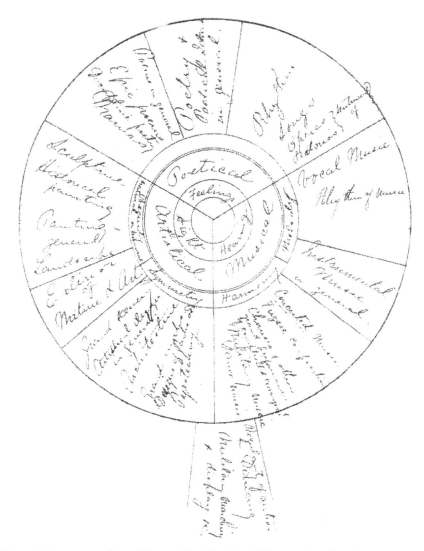

Figure 1 A representation of Jevons' classification of the arts, based on the senses on which the works of art operate, with a double hierarchy: the level of abstractness (getting less abstract from the centre to the outer edge of the circle) and the intellectual significance (getting lower when moving from top to bottom).

part of the emotions does not fit into this framework, but even these emotions are closely dependent on the three categories mentioned. Finally, Jevons introduces a table (which we investigate later in this section).

The first part of the chapter makes clear that the manuscript belongs to Jevons' larger project of the 'science of man'. Music is not merely an instrument of pleasure, it is an essential part of every human being. The aim of the 'Functions' chapter is to identify the precise place that music occupies among the activities of a person. Everyone should experience the feelings that originate from listening to a piece of music from time to time, because these feelings let us forget the daily sorrows. Moreover, they lead to the experience of a certain 'moral strength' that enables us to survive in the context of the difficulties of our lives. All this may suggest that music should merely be seen as a 'tranquilizer' of the mind, an interpretation to be found elsewhere.[79] Although this aspect is certainly present, a first nuance of this statement should be that it is an *essential* 'tranquilizer', which is necessary for every person. But more important, music is not a simple instrument of pleasure, because the feeling that is associated with the music has a certain intellectual dimension.

This becomes clear in the text under consideration when Jevons states that music is not equally important for everyone, and when he argues that everyone already experiences the feelings associated with music to a greater or less degree. Although Jevons maintains that these feelings have nothing at all to do with reason or knowledge, there has to be something 'intellectual', which implies that some people enjoy music more than other people, and that it is more important in some people's lives than in other's. We can clarify this point by taking other sources into account. Jevons states that it is possible to understand and appreciate music without being able to play it brilliantly. This indicates that this ability does not stem from some manual or technical abilities. Jevons compares playing music with reading poetry (Black 1973: 257). Elsewhere, he even writes:

> I regard a fine piece of music like a fine poem, or essay or philosophical work, that is as a thing to be studied, understood and remembered. In this point of view playing music though it may *bore* others is still as good an employment of time *to a certain extent* as reading.
>
> (Black 1973: 225, original emphasis)

This quotation clarifies Jevons' statement in the manuscript that, although the feelings associated with the contemplation of scientific, ethical or religious subjects are somewhat feebler than the feelings associated with music, they still have intellectual superiority. The study of art forms is similar to scientific study, but emotionally stronger and intellectually lower. Moreover, we show below that art forms that are concerned with subjects that may also become topics of scientific investigation are valued higher in Jevons' utilitarian framework. All this implies that Jevons attributes an important intellectual dimension to art and music. A closer reading of other letters indicates that there are really different kinds of music, which are associated with different kinds of persons. Jevons writes about Handel's *Israel in Egypt*:

> As you are aware it consists of little except grand heavy choruses describing the plagues of Egypt and the Exodus of the Israelites. The subject is one perhaps which no writer but Handel dared to attempt; ordinary music and ordinary art usually appeal to the more common and immediate feelings of

the heart, which every one comprehends more or less. To paint such feelings or describe them in poetry is no very difficult thing, but as it is only the very greatest artists that can reproduce historical scenes, or embody things with which the mind always associates vague ideas of extreme grandeur, so it is only the highest master-hand that could take music from its ordinary sphere, and make it describe events of strange and miraculous nature as those which are the subject of Israel.

(JA10/1/40a)

This quotation indicates that Jevons regards this 'descriptive music', which reproduces historical scenes with 'extreme grandeur', as a high form of music. Jevons' letters to Henrietta are filled with descriptions of parts of musical pieces that express, for instance, the movement of frogs or the falling of hail (JA10/1/40a) and, elsewhere, Jevons describes a passage which 'reaches the ultimatum of expression, the difference of Heaven and Hell. It is the highest effect of art' (JA10/1/37c).[80] This indicates that a real masterpiece deals with historical or religious subjects, which are reproduced emotionally in the inner eye (or ear) of the reader. This explains the lower status of music in comparison with science or religion: although they deal with similar subjects, science or religion are concerned with the contemplation of these subjects themselves, whereas music merely reproduces feelings of grandeur that are associated with these subjects. Although the latter feelings are more forceful than those produced by scientific or religious contemplation, they still remain intellectually at a lower level. Jevons' emphasis on the intellectual content of music also implies that, although strictly speaking no knowledge is required to appreciate a masterpiece, some knowledge may help. A person completely unfamiliar with the biblical or historical scenes reproduced in the piece will not be able to perceive the intellectual significance of the music. He might be able to discover the beauty of the piece as such, but he could not relate it to the occurrences that Jevons describes in his letters. This point is reinforced in a manuscript to be found in the Henrietta section at the John Rylands library (JA10/1/32b), which appears to be an earlier draft of part of the 'Functions' chapter that is not in the archives.[81] Jevons writes:

Music, on the other hand, never attains its highest pitch of beauty and interest unless accompanied by words which giving a *poetical* meaning to its otherwise inanimate expression, intensify as well as define its influence on the mind. All the greatest musical compositions are, I believe, *vocal.*

(JA10/1/32b)

All this implies that Jevons considers music to be more than simply a 'tranquilizer' for the mind. It has an intellectual and religious dimension. But there exist different kinds of' 'higher and lower' forms of music, and not every person has a similar need for music of high quality. We have already stated above that Jevons does not consider himself to be a scientific genius who creates scientific inventions, but he thinks that his ability consists of developing already existing ideas into something symmetrical. Ordinary people, on the contrary, may not be at all suited for intellectual work, and should therefore confine themselves to routine labour. A similar picture emerges in Jevons' view on music. A musical genius creates high forms of music, as we saw earlier. Jevons does not consider himself to be a musical genius, but he is able to play and appreciate the higher forms of music in his way. Ordinary people, on the other hand, may only be able to enjoy the lowest and simple forms of music which are immediately clear to anybody (resulting from a natural propensity of every human being). We return to this issue when we discuss Jevons' critique of Alison (who neglects the difference between higher and lower forms of music) and when we discuss Jevons' policy prescriptions regarding public performances of music.

At any rate, Jevons does not distinguish clearly the intellectual from the non-intellectual aspects of music. The feelings associated with music belong to the perception, and not to the reason, and this may explain why they are in fact inexplicable. Although they do not depend on knowledge, there is certainly a connection between emotions and knowledge that is not stated clearly. Instead, the concept of 'perceptive pleasure' serves to cover this tension in Jevons' music theory. In the first place, it seems strange that Jevons includes in his definition of 'perceptive pleasure' emotions arising through the medium of the mind. He does not recognize explicitly that, when the 'mind' is at stake, intellectual aspects will certainly interfere. In the second place, he writes that there is no 'necessary exercise of the higher faculties of reason', but he does not exclude the possibility that reason may interfere. And, finally, the feelings arising out of the contemplation of scientific, religious or scientific subjects are somewhat similar, but feebler. The concept of 'perceptive pleasure' covers this tension, which is also present in Jevons' diagrams depicting his classification of the arts.

The Jevons archives contain three separate diagrams: JA6/45/4, JA6/45/5, JA10/1/32b. They are classified in different sections of the archives, but it is highly probable that Jevons does not refer to one of these diagrams in his chapter on the functions of music, but to a similar (missing) table instead. Jevons writes that the diagram is represented on the following page, but this page is missing. However, no doubt remains that these diagrams express the classification that Jevons refers to in his description. Jevons sums up the classes of art that he differentiates with regard to the senses on which they operate. He establishes a natural distinction between the sense of hearing, the sense of seeing and a so far unnamed sense, a 'third and highest division', in which he places poetical ideas or mental pictures of beauty. For each of these senses, Jevons then intends to sum up the several subclasses of subjects and objects. The three diagrams represent three different versions of the same classification. JA6/45/5 and JA10/1/32b are simple tables; the elaborate diagram JA6/45/4 is reproduced in the Appendix (Figure 1). All diagrams contain sight and hearing as main classes; the name of the third class varies. JA6/45/5 mentions 'memory and understanding', JA10/1/32b 'mind and feeling' and JA6/45/4 simply 'feelings'. All three diagrams mention a small fourth class of motion (marching, dancing), which we reconsider below.

In the 'Functions' chapter, Jevons seems to refer to one of the tables, because he writes that 'poetical ideas' form the central and main division but, because of their close connection with 'natural objects', this last column is placed alongside in a column under the heading 'sight'. On either side are placed the artificial representations of these objects and ideas, by both sight and hearing. This is precisely the structure of the two tables JA6/45/5 and JA10/1/32b: in both cases, the columns are named (1) 'sight art', (2) 'sight nature', (3) 'memory and understanding' or 'mind and feeling', (4) 'hearing' and (5) 'motion'. Jevons stresses that the tables provide insights into the close connection between the different forms of perceptive pleasures. For example, 'landscape and painting in general', 'natural scenery', 'descriptive poetry' and 'descriptive music' are placed at the same height in both tables. We show later that the additional material (JA10/1/32b) elaborates on the similarities between the different art forms, but it is highly improbable that Jevons refers to one of the tables in the manuscript (JA6/47/8). In the 'Functions' chapter, Jevons refers to a column 'Poetical Ideas', and not to 'memory and understanding' nor to 'mind and feeling'. All this suggests that he refers to a table with a similar layout to both tables from the archives (JA6/45/5 and JA10/1/32b), but not to one of these tables themselves.

The different layout of JA6/45/4 suggests a different approach to the classification. Many other differences substantiate this claim. Under the heading of sight, the tables mention a division between art and nature, whereas the diagram has no such division. In this last case, the 'exterior of nature and art' is mentioned as one of several subclasses. In the category of sight, the diagram makes mention of a division between 'beauty' and 'symmetry', whereas the other tables do not. A section on 'Harmony of colours' does not appear in the diagram, nor do 'ballads'. 'Oratories and opera' are classified under the class of feelings in diagram JA6/45/4, instead of under hearing. This diagram also contains a division between 'harmony' and 'melody' under the section on hearing, whereas the tables do not. Although there cannot be any certainty on this issue, it seems reasonable to suppose that the more elaborate diagram JA6/45/4 should be seen as the latest and most definitive version, and we therefore decided to reproduce this diagram in the Appendix. We take special interest in two aspects of the classification: the structure of the diagrams and the way of presenting concrete art forms and objects. We take JA6/45/4 as the main focus of our attention and refer to differences from or similarities to the other two tables when required. We argue that all three diagrams contain a hierarchy of 'levels of abstractness', but only diagram JA6/45/4 contains an elaborate second hierarchy that expresses the intellectual significance of the different forms of art. The tables are rather intended to represent similarities, as we argued above.

The general structure of Jevons' tables and diagram seems very clear. He presents a classification of art forms on the basis of abstract categories of perception. By inferring such abstract characteristics of perception from concrete art forms, Jevons is able to construct a hierarchical view on the perception of art. At the centre of the diagram (or the top for the other two), we find the most general divisions. These are also the most abstract instances of perception of art. The more we approach the outer edge of the circle, the more concrete the perceptions become: poems, paintings and choruses are more sensible than beauty, melody or harmony. Jevons uses the biological origin of the perception as the criterion to classify different kinds of perceptive pleasures. Hearing is not seeing because we don't see with our ears. In between, however, Jevons looks for a denominator as general as possible. He comes up with the concepts of 'symmetry' and 'beauty' under the general heading 'artistical' for sight, and the concepts of 'harmony' and 'melody' under the general heading 'musical' for hearing. He does not succeed in mentioning a similar term for the category of feeling, although 'poetical' is placed under this heading. Further from the centre of the circle, we find more sensible examples of the arts: under the heading 'beauty', Jevons recognizes, among others, 'sculpture' and 'painting'; under 'symmetry', he places for instance 'grand scenery' and 'architecture'. The 'exterior of nature and art' separates beauty from symmetry, which apparently indicates that it possesses the characteristics of both categories. Under 'melody', Jevons places, among others, 'vocal music', and under 'harmony', he places for instance 'military music'. Under the category 'poetical', Jevons places 'poetry', 'rhythm' and 'opera', as the most sensible examples of the class of poetical ideas. The furthest from the centre of the diagram is the category of 'regularity of motion', including 'dancing', 'military marching' and 'military display'. These very sensible art forms, on the overlap between sight and hearing, do produce as much emotion as any other, but cannot be represented directly by one of the three main classes. At first sight, Jevons seems to classify art forms through their 'levels of abstractness'. The individual is at the centre of the diagram; he is surrounded by different kinds of senses and the perceptive pleasures with which they are associated; and the events capable of producing these pleasures are listed at the outer edge of the circle.

However, there is also another hierarchical structure in Jevons' classification: from top to bottom. It visualizes a classification on the basis of Jevons' most problematic conception, namely the intellectual characteristics of art. We have already argued above that, although Jevons states that music may be a tranquilizer of the mind, he clearly maintains some intellectual aspects. Jevons remains vague in his conceptualization of this intellectual function, but a close examination of the diagrams reveals that they refer to it. The intellectual hierarchy may even be said to govern the structure of diagram JA6/45/4. The top of the circle diagram presents the art forms which, in Jevons' opinion, require the most intellectual perception. The more we approach the bottom, the more the art forms become less intellectually stimulating. Following this classification, a hierarchy from poetry through visual arts and music to motional art forms becomes visible. The best example may be the higher rank of 'melody' over 'harmony', as it reflects the intellectual superiority of 'melody'. Jevons writes in Chapter 3 of the music manuscript, 'On Melody':

> Harmony, indeed in some inscrutable manner *pleases* the *ear*; melody appeals to the *mind*, and it is merely by a succession of sounds, rising or falling, or varied in an infinite number of ways, that the musical composer has to

express his thought and feelings and give that *meaning* or *soul* to his sounds which constitutes their intrinsic value.

(JA6/47/7)

This is perhaps the most explicit statement on the intellectual 'cleavage' in Jevons' thought on music. A melody is a meaningful collection of words, as a book is a meaningful collection of sentences. Melody appeals to the 'mind' and expresses 'thoughts', but the feelings associated with it nevertheless fall under the class of 'perceptive pleasures'. Although Jevons does not recognize these intellectual aspects explicitly, he ranks 'intellectually higher' art forms above 'intellectual lower' forms. Other examples from the class of music provide the same insights. Jevons places vocal music (opera, songs, oratories) on a higher level than instrumental music. We have already seen above that Jevons prefers vocal music, as it depicts descriptive scenes (of historical significance) which require a more intellectual attitude and perception. The only exception in the distinction between vocal and instrumental music, the choruses, reinforces this argument. Jevons considers choral music outside the opera of less intellectual importance because it operates mainly within the context of less cerebral manifestations and grand performances. The same 'intellectual cleavage' explains why 'historical painting' is ranked above 'painting in general' and 'landscape', and why 'pyrotechny' receives a low hierarchical status. Similarly, the low position of the motional class outside the diagram, on the overlap between symmetry and harmony, not only gives utterance to its insignificance on a perceptive level of abstraction, but also on that of intellectual perception.

This second classification reinforces our point that the diagram reproduced in the Appendix contains the most definitive and structural view on Jevons' classification. The other tables contain the (first) abstraction hierarchy, but they do not visualize thoroughly the intellectual degree (the second hierarchy). The tables do express some hierarchies of this kind, such as the superiority of 'descriptive music' over 'vocal music and melody and general', but they do not express more general hierarchies (e.g. the poetical, artistical and musical are placed alongside in the tables). Moreover, the fact that the two tables mention 'memory and understanding' and 'mind and feelings', respectively, suggests that, in the earlier tables, Jevons was not fully aware of the intellectual 'cleavage' in his classification. The final diagram mentions only 'feelings', which may indicate that Jevons tried to demarcate perceptive pleasures more clearly from intellectual activities. He could not, of course, annihilate this tension by simply changing a concept, but the more detailed visualization of the 'second hierarchy' brings more clarity to the classification. Whereas the tables emphasize the similarities between the different forms of perceptive pleasures, the diagram puts a stronger emphasis on the 'intellectual hierarchy' of different feelings.

The additional music material to be found in the Henrietta section at the John Rylands Library (JA10/1/32b, see above) complements Jevons' classification of the arts, and plays down the strictness of his divisions. In this manuscript, Jevons elaborates on the hierarchy of the arts:

Music is the pleasurable exercise of one of our senses and in this view stands in the same rank as the other two divisions of perceptive pleasures. It must be allowed however that if we consider the comparative values of the three kinds of perceptive pleasures that the balance is somewhat against our Musical Art, as being more abstract and of less general meaning and appliance than the visual and poetical dimensions of Art. It is not like these latter occupied with subjects for instance nature or man the contemplations of which in a scientific, metaphysical or other point of view are of much superior importance and interest. Hence Art and Poetry must be allowed to take precedence, not that they are in themselves better or more easy sources of *perceptive* enjoyment but because they are likely to lead the mind to higher pursuits and more valuable acquirements.

(JA10/1/32b)

This quotation indicates once more that music, and art in general, have an intellectual dimension that is somewhat covered in the concept of 'perceptive pleasure'. Whereas 'descriptive music' is more important to Jevons because it reproduces historical and religious scenes of 'beauty and grandeur', art and poetry should take precedence over music because their subjects may be investigated scientifically as well. In this sense, art may become the first step for the mind to become interested in scientific investigations. However, Jevons continues by arguing that 'more fairness' should be brought into this comparison. If the money that was spent in erecting a building of 'architectural beautification' were instead to have been invested in the maintenance of a small staff of musicians that would perform publicly and gratuitously, the town might be more pleasant and beautiful than in the first case (JA10/1/32b). The argument that the public performance of music is rather inexpensive is an important one; it returns in Jevons' writings on the policy of public performances (see below). Moreover, these writings confirm once more that the music manuscript is part of the larger 'science of man' project. In a typically utilitarian fashion, Jevons balances the costs and benefits of several forms of 'perceptive pleasures' against each other. Moreover, Jevons underlines the importance of artistic expressions for the 'science of man': although the production of objects with an agreeable and beautiful shape 'is entirely useless in an utilitarian point of view, still in all ages much attention has been given to it, and more and more value depended upon it as he [man] became more and more refined' (JA10/1/32b). The performance of art in a culture therefore expresses its level of civilization.

The additional material also contains some arguments regarding the incompleteness of Jevons' divisions. A 'new but insignificant class of motional perceptive pleasures' is formed by joining the idea of rhythm in music with regularity of motion, as in marching and dancing (JA10/1/32b). We have already stated above that this small class is depicted at the bottom in Jevons' diagram: it is not included in one of the three main divisions, and the fact that it appears at the bottom of the diagram illustrates its low status in Jevons' classification. Indeed, elsewhere (in 1878), Jevons reports that he always considered dancing to be something vulgar, until he learned from his visits to Denmark that this was a prejudice against this art form:

> But we are so accustomed to see ballet girls in evanescent skirts, in ambiguous attitudes, or dressed up as wasps or cupids, or something extravagant and low in taste, that we have established an inseparable association of ideas between dancing and immorality. I retain a grateful recollection of the Froeken Carey, who opened my eyes more than anything else to the degradation of public taste in England. I afterwards learned that Copenhagen is considered a great school of graceful and chaste dancing.
>
> (Jevons 1883: 22)

Besides the introduction of this 'new and insignificant class', Jevons plays down the strictness of his classification by arguing that several classes may be joined to form sensations that may not belong entirely to one of the three main divisions. Poetry is usually rhythmical and may be joined with the sounds of a melody; and opera should be seen as a combination of poetry, music and artistical representation (JA10/1/32b). The three main divisions can even be defined by reference to each other:

> Poetry is the Artistical or Melodious Arrangement of Ideas.
> Art is the Poetical Arrangement of Natural Objects.
> Music is the Poetical or Artistical Arrangement of Sounds.
>
> (JA10/1/32b)

Jevons' divisions should therefore not be taken too strictly. There is also no strict hierarchy among these divisions: music is more abstract, and therefore less likely to lead the mind to subjects of scientific interest but, on the other hand, music is not expensive, more universal and better suited for many different occasions, and it does not require much concentration and reflection (JA10/1/32b). Similar arguments can be found in Jevons' utilitarian judgement of public performances of music (see below). But there is still an 'intellectual cleavage' in Jevons' music theory, when he argues that the 'lower' forms of music are easily accessible to everyone, whereas the possibility of appreciating 'higher' forms depends on the formation of the ear. This 'cleavage' appears in Jevons' discussion of Alison's *Essays in Taste*, which is to be found at the end of the additional material JA10/1/32b. A review of Jevons' remarks on Alison is also a good starting point for an investigation of the relation between Jevons' music manuscript and other writings on music, art and aesthetics in his time.

The music manuscript in context

We have already mentioned that the intellectual 'cleavage' in Jevons' writings on music is especially visible in his arguments regarding the intellectual superiority of melody over harmony. Precisely this argument forms the core of Jevons' criticism on Archibald Alison's *Essays on the Nature and Principles of Taste*, published in 1790. Although Alison distinguishes between different kinds of sounds, he does not establish a hierarchy in Jevons' sense, nor does he emphasize the necessity of musical training and education for the adequate perception of higher forms of music. According to Alison, all sounds may be sublime, although not to the same extent. The level of sublimity of each sound or series of sounds depends on the precise nature of the sound (thunder, tempest, cascade), but also on the association the perceiver makes. Alison acknowledges that not every perceiver has the same ability to form such associations, and is not equally sensible to the sublimity of sounds (Alison 1790: 153). He attributes these differences to several reasons, such as for instance the temper of the perceiver or the regularity of occurrence. A musical composition affects the emotions of sublimity or beauty as a result of the nature of the single sounds, the nature of the whole composition or the associations the listener connects with it. According to Alison, the ability to create associations is the key in the perception of music (Alison 1790: 194–5).

Jevons criticizes Alison for not establishing a firm hierarchy of different kinds of music: whereas rhythm and harmony may be experienced by everyone, the proper appreciation of melody requires a genuine formation of the ear. He writes:

> He [Alison] has not sufficiently entered on the Theory of Music, to see the complete distinctions of melody, rhythm and harmony, which all contribute to the pleasures of music, but independently of each other [. . .] Still if anything more were required to prove the independence of associated feelings, we may be convinced by the fact that rhythm and harmony are naturally discriminated and enjoyed by all persons and at all ages, while the enjoyment of a melody depends absolutely on the character and education of the hearer.
>
> (JA10/1/32b)

Whereas Jevons relates the sense for higher art forms to training and education, Alison refers to the aesthetic categories of the beautiful and the sublime. Jevons refers to these concepts as well, but does not put much emphasis on them because of his utilitarian orientation (see below). According to Alison, the perception of art is attended with a specific pleasurable emotion, incomparable to other emotions. This particular emotion is then called taste. But, unlike other emotions, taste has a particular interaction with the mind:

> Taste is that Faculty of the human Mind, by which we perceive and enjoy, whatever is BEAUTIFUL or SUBLIME in the works of Nature or Art.
>
> (Alison 1790: vii)

Although Alison tries to connect taste with the human mind, he does not elaborate on the function of the mind in the act of perception. Alison tries to isolate what he calls the most important elements of the pleasurable perception: the aesthetic concepts of the sublime and the beautiful. When the artist tries to strive for truly great art that is permanent and genial, he has to employ the concepts of the sublime and the beautiful. Throughout his essays, however, Alison hardly succeeds in isolating the pleasures associated with beauty or sublimity from other pleasures. On the whole, he seems to be unable to connect the emotion of pleasure with the effect it has on the human mind. Rather, his use of the sublime and the beautiful as acknowledged intellectual concepts keep him from bridging the gap between emotion and intellect.

Alison's vocabulary of the beauty and the sublime belongs to a specific Anglo-Saxon aesthetic tradition that considers the sublime to be the ultimate goal and structure that governs the arts. That goal is the attempt to find a natural foundation of the perception of the arts, and of taste. One of the most prominent pioneers of this tradition is the third Earl of Shaftesbury. His contribution not only deals with the specific characteristics of sublimity, especially in its connection with the religiosity of art, but also, and perhaps more importantly, with the attempt to find a natural and anthropological foundation of the sublime. Shaftesbury was a pupil of John Locke, and tried to incorporate his empiricism into aesthetic enquiries. As such, he is one of the first who tried to establish an empiricist foundation of sublimity. His view of mankind as harmonious and virtuous was, in the early eighteenth century, particularly reflected in classical architecture and music (especially in the proportionality of the sonata). In short, Shaftesbury argued that mankind is good by nature, and therefore able to recognize other good aspects in the world (such as the works of nature and true art). Shaftesbury's empiricism implies that this recognition is based on the senses. Although his influence remains implicit and vague, his views on the subject of the foundation of aesthetics have been of great importance for the further development of thought on art and music (Shaftesbury 1790).[82] Alison tried to complete Shaftesbury's empiricist foundation by combining it with his emphasis on the intellectual aspects of the perception of art. He enlarged Shaftesbury's concept by adding, apart from the sensorial recognition, the appeal to the mind as well (Kallich 1948). We have already argued that Alison introduces the categories of the sublime and the beautiful for this purpose, but he does not succeed in bridging the gap between emotion and intellect.

Alison's conceptualization brings Jevons to mind. Both use the same vocabulary and adhere to the same established tradition of aesthetics. Like Alison, Jevons recognizes the importance of the concepts of sublimity and the beautiful, especially when he refers to the difference between the intellectual and non-intellectual characteristics of aesthetical perception:

> [A certain feeling] is excited by the contemplation of subjects of <u>Interest Beauty</u> or <u>Sublimity</u> [. . .] It arises in short from the <u>contemplation</u> of anything possessing a degree of fresh <u>interest beauty or grandeur.</u>
>
> (JA6/47/8)

Precisely in this section, in which Jevons tries to define or describe the feeling he perceives when confronted with great objects of art, he resorts to the terms connected with the Anglo-Saxon tradition. But while Alison clearly places himself within this tradition and tries to continue it, Jevons does not consider aesthetical concepts as essential for an investigation of its effects on the mind and emotions. This may be explained by Jevons' utilitarian approach to the subject. Whereas Alison would like to enlarge Shaftesbury's empiristic foundation of aesthetics by taking intellectual aspects into account, Jevons would like to examine the 'use' of music in the context of the 'science of man'. Jevons wants to know the precise place of music among man's occupations, and he would like to develop utilitarian guidelines for using music. Many of the writings on art from the middle of the nineteenth century onwards treat art in a utilitarian way.[83] Resulting from a desire to preserve art (or deal with it) in a more industrialized society, the main argument is that, if nothing else, art serves as an educator of man, to make him perceptive of nature and the beauty in it. Evidently, this argument is connected strongly with a moralist view on the matter. Jevons is therefore not so much interested in the nature of the sublime as such but, rather, in the capability of art to raise the level of morality. This is especially visible in Jevons' writings on what we might call the 'political economy of music'. In the next section, we show that these writings are compatible with our examination of the music manuscript. Although written more than twenty years after the manuscript, it may be seen as a policy outcome of Jevons' ideas on aesthetics.

The political economy of music

We showed earlier that Jevons uses utilitarian notions in his comparison of different art forms. Several of Jevons' arguments return in his article 'Amusements of the People', which originally appeared in the *Contemporary Review* of 1878 and was reprinted in *Methods of Social Reform* (1883). In this essay, Jevons complains about the attitudes of lower class people in England. He argues that the behaviour of drunken English 'blackguards' differs fundamentally from the behaviour of Continental or American lower class people, who are, 'comparatively speaking', ladies and gentlemen of refinement. Jevons states that it is difficult to change these bad habits, especially because they have been confirmed by centuries of ignorance and mistaken legislation. Lower class people in England do not have access to good moral public amusements and, therefore, their only option is to get drunk in their spare time and to cause trouble. In Continental Europe, these morally elevating amusements exist, and this explains why the lower class people in these countries have a much more refined behaviour. In England, on the contrary, the aristocracy suppressed the existing amusements, but did not offer alternatives. The earlier amusements had to be suppressed, as they were but covers for crime and immorality, but the people are in need of new amusements instead. Lower class people are mostly excluded from natural enjoyments because they do not have any property, and the existing public amusements are usually too expensive. The aristocracy lives a life of amusements, and the hard-working labourers should get a harmless and healthy counterpart. This should give rise to moral improvement of the lower classes, through a change of habits and attitudes (Jevons 1883: 2–7).

Jevons has two purposes in mind: entertainment and civilization of the people. Both purposes are interconnected, because the necessary entertainment of the people should lead their habits in a more civilized direction. Especially music seems to be the best means of popular recreation, as it fulfils all the requirements. Jevons lists three arguments that are similar to his earlier remarks regarding the utility of music in relation to other forms of art (see above). First, listening to music involves no bodily fatigue. No efforts are required, only a 'passive abandonment of the mind to the train of ideas and emotions suggested by the strains' (Jevons 1883: 9). Other possibilities, such as visiting galleries or museums, involve rather tiring body movements and are therefore less suited for the purposes of entertainment and civilization. A second main argument is the low cost of music. The cost of a theatre is necessarily higher than the cost of a music performance, because theatre is drama plus the music. Institutions that are designed for higher class people generally cost more, which necessitates a higher entrance fee. Thirdly, music is purer and more removed from concrete life than a drama. This is important because the public performance should distract the labourers from their daily work and sorrows. Jevons recognizes that there exist 'lascivious' songs, but the impurity lies in the words, not in the music (Jevons 1883: 8–11). This clarifies Jevons' statement in the music manuscript about the attainment of 'a sort of confident moral strength': the music serves as a 'tranquilizer' of the mind (entertainment), but the songs have to be pure and morally elevating (civilization). All this is also compatible with the importance that Jevons attaches to music that reproduces scenes of historical and religious grandeur, and it illustrates the importance that Jevons attaches to vocal music. We conclude once again that, while music does serve as a 'tranquilizer', it should contain an intellectual and moral component in order to elevate the moral attitude of the listener. This would also annihilate the unhealthy habits of lower class people:

> What some seek at the cost of health, and life, and reputation, from alcohol, and from opium, that they might obtain innocuously from music, if they could cultivate true musical taste.
>
> (Jevons 1883: 10)

The cultivation of musical taste is therefore a prerequisite for the moral elevation of the people. Jevons argues that the low quality of musical education among the masses explains their 'helpless state' when seeking recreation. Their musical education should somehow be 'triggered' by the organization of free public musical performances. As this would not cost too much, there are no real financial burdens. Middle- and upper class people are, however, afraid that these performances will attract 'a horrid crowd of roughs and pickpockets'. But as soon as 'the novelty of the thing had worn off' and the roughs and the pickpockets would stay away because of the presence of the police, middle-class people would no longer be reluctant to go to these performances and bring their families with them. Moreover, higher and upper class people might be willing to pay for reserved chairs or by a subscription list, and this would possibly cover the expenses. The performances should be organized by local movements. Jevons claims that religious and sacred music is especially important, and it may be attained by people from all ranks. The elevation of the tastes of the poorer classes should be achieved by a mixture of different kinds of music: the better class of dance music, old English songs and popular classical songs, but a careful intermixture is certainly appropriate. Jevons seems to suggest that people would be attracted by the more popular and easier parts of the performance, and that the careful injection of some 'higher' musical pieces would gradually raise the musical tastes. Jevons' own observation is that every person is able to appreciate a really beautiful melody; only musical symphonies require a long training (Jevons 1883: 11–16). This is in accordance with Jevons' earlier views, as in his criticism of Alison discussed above.

The government cannot interfere directly in the private organization of already existing music halls; the audience has to demand better entertainment. On the other hand, the already existing public places of recreation (the Crystal and Alexandra Palaces and the Westminster Aquarium) should maintain a high tone in order to avoid degradation to a vulgar level but, meanwhile, they have to 'make a point of mingling all classes together' (Jevons 1883: 17–18). This argument resembles Jevons' discussion of trade unions in *The State in Relation to Labour*, where he raises hands for heterogeneous co-operations. A partnership binding together the interests of employer and workman should be the solution to the labour problem. Industrial divisions should be perpendicular, not horizontal: the workman's interests should be bound up with those of his employer's. The workman will then become a shareholder in the firm (Jevons 1882: 143–9). A careful intermixture of higher and lower class people would give rise to moral improvement, on the work floor as well as at public performances. In this sense, Jevons remarks that those who would like to elevate the tastes of the masses place the means to achieve this goal as far away as possible from these masses (Jevons 1883: 18). A proper method of improving habits and morality should, on the contrary, be that higher class people visit popular performances in order to give a good example that may be imitated by lower class people (Jevons 1883: 24). Middle-class people love to imitate their betters, but they should also be willing to visit 'lower' performances. The careful intermixture of classes would give rise to social improvement through 'aping the upper-class'. Jevons writes at the end of his essay:

> There are none so blind as they who will not see, and this is the kind of blindness which prevents us from seeing that the vulgarity of the cheap trip, the inanity of the music-hall, and the general low tone of popular manners, are no necessary characteristics of hard hands and short purses, but are due to the way in which for so long a time popular education and popular recreation have been discountenanced. Of course the question of recreation is subordinate to that of education.
>
> (Jevons 1883: 26)

The last sentence once more shows that the intellectual and moral aspects of music are more important than its recreative function. Jevons' policy prescriptions are not limited to the case of music; several other policies with an even greater emphasis on intellectual aspects are present in *Methods of Social Reform*. We have already discussed Jevons' policy proposals for libraries and museums in the previous chapter. However, Jevons' educational project struggles with some difficulties, as *The Spectator* remarks in October 1878:[84]

> Mr. Jevons' advice to give the people music may be sound, but where is the evidence that the people wish for it, in place of more objectionable entertainment? Why, in fact, does not the people, if it would like music, subscribe its twopences, and have music?
>
> (Black 1977b: 291)

This criticism points to a vicious circle in Jevons' policy prescriptions: he would like to alter the musical taste of the masses through public performances of music but, in order to be able to appreciate refined forms of music, a certain musical taste already has to be present. People might be more attracted to lower and possibly more 'vulgar' forms of music because of their bad tastes, whereas precisely 'higher' forms of music would be required to improve morality. Here, we encounter the 'cleavage' in Jevons' music theory already identified above. The music manuscript we examined earlier refines this observation. It is clear that Jevons has a somewhat solitary, intellectual and high-class conception of music. He prefers descriptive music that recreates biblical and historical scenes of beauty and grandeur for the listener. A piece of music should be studied like a book; it should be understood and remembered. This conception of music (or art in general) indeed allows moral elevation, and also intellectual elevation if the theme of the art work may become a subject of scientific investigation as well. The concept of 'perceptive pleasure' covers the tension between the intellectual and emotional aspects of music, and is not a valid analytical concept for differentiating 'higher' from 'lower' forms of music. It is unclear whether a 'careful intermixture' of different kinds of music (and classes) is possible.

Here, we encounter a general problem in Jevons' thought. White (1994b) elaborates on a general 'cleavage' in Jevons' political economy between the individual of the theory and the character of a concrete person. This is especially visible in Jevons' discussion of the reduction in working hours, which he opposed. A reduction in working hours would only give rise to greater drunkenness. Moreover, the majority of the population (labourers, artisans, white-collar workers) would prefer 'greater ease' when wages are rising wages, whereas a small exceptional class of 'learned professionals' would work harder when incomes are increasing. Jevons' economic theory is constructed around the notion of a 'representative individual' but, in his practical surveys, terms of class and character should bridge the gap between theoretical agent and concrete individuals. The 'representative individual' is based on Jevons' image of the Victorian middle class: the labourer in Jevons' theory would, in the absence of other motives, devote all energy to the accumulation of wealth. As this definition does not fit in the case of lower class people, Jevons' description of character and class behaviour relaxes his '*ceteris paribus'* definition of the labourer. Different solutions for economic problems emerge when different characters are involved.[85] In this case, Jevons' intellectual, solitary and upper class conception of music may be ill suited to the problem of the elevation of the taste of the aggregate of low-class people.[86]

Conclusion

Our reading of Jevons' music manuscript confirms once more that his large oeuvre should be considered as a unified whole. Jevons' utilitarian project of the 'science of man' consists of many surveys from several disciplines, including the 'science and art of music'. His general methodology entails the construction of a (representative or average) individual, and application of this notion to a concrete case by taking elements of 'character' into account. In the case of music, the manuscript may be seen as the toolbox in which the individual perceiver is created. This individual is then used in Jevons' 'Amusements of the People'. Unfortunately, Jevons' solitary and intellectual conception of music seems not to be suited to an elevation of the morality of the masses. A vicious circle between taste and training becomes visible.

Appendix 1: JA6/47/8

Chapter 'On the Functions of Music'

By functions of music is partly meant what one should call the <u>use</u> of music, but not exactly so. If we were to speak of <u>using</u> music, we should imply that it was a sort of instrument, one of pleasure no doubt, which we could employ or may avoid at will.

But music is more than this; it is an integral part of a man, of the musician of course more especially, but of all men more or less; they could not lay it aside any more than they could one of the perceptions or faculties of their minds when once developed; and they use it by nature as they use any of their senses, rather than as an instrument supplied by art. By 'functions' of music then is meant more exactly the part or position occupied by it among the occupations & capacities of men.

Before attempting to explain what I believe the part of music really to be, I must call upon the reader to bring before his mind as distinctly as possible a certain feeling that all have no doubt been conscious of, to a greater or less degree, on innumerable occasions. It is excited by the contemplation of subjects of <u>Interest</u> <u>Beauty</u> or <u>Sublimity</u>, and consists of a gentle excitement, an engrossment of the thoughts by agreeable subjects and a general removal of the mind from its ordinary course of duties & frailties, and its continual mixture of slight pleasures and plains.

When rising to an unusual pitch, the feeling of which I speak becomes an intense delight; it absorbs the attention completely, and causing it to forget ordinary affairs and thoughts, elevates it to a region of pleasurable sensations nowhere else discovered. It is indefinite however, leads to no conclusion, suggests it may almost be said no leading or strong thought or purpose and even of one's future path in life, or unavoidable duties happen to occur to the mind in the midst of this sort of intoxication, they appear smoother than ever before, the difficulties have entirely vanished and <u>oneself</u> feels such a sort of confident moral strength, as will only too soon be found to disappear when this state of feeling has ended and the petty or great difficulties of life once again visible in all their reality. Who that has attended a concert, play or other public performance, has not experienced this sudden and almost disgusting <u>revulsion</u> of feelings at its termination when the music has finally ceased & no longer rivets the attention, and a dreamy progress home, and a renewed circle of duties and the sorrow are all that seem to await one.

This feeling, too, is often excited more or less, by every pleasant country walk, by sight-seeing by beautiful and extensive views or grand and striking scenery on sea or land, by magnificent architectural or engineering works or a fine piece of poetry, or lastly by <u>music</u> whether in the wonderfully grand and sublime Oratories or the sweet and exciting Song. It arises in short from the <u>contemplation</u> of anything possessing a degree of fresh <u>interest beauty or grandeur</u> and is accompanied by cheerfulness or good humour, often rising to excitement or a sense of impressiveness. Let the reader bring to his recollection as many occasions as possible when this has been felt and by a short reflection try to obtain as clear and definite an idea of its nature as he possibly can.

To investigate its cause would be to enter one of the most difficult and least certain of metaphysical subjects and be quite beyond our purposes. It will suffice to say that it does not depend in any particular degree on knowledge. A pile of rocks is no grander in this point of view after their geology has been examined, the beauty of a forest scene is not increased by a botanical acquaintance with the trees and plants composing it, nor is a knowledge of <u>colouring</u> or <u>harmonical composition necessary</u> for the enjoyment of excellent painting or music, though no doubt all knowledge & such acquirements refine the mind and tend to make it more susceptible of such impressions. A large & well-designed piece of architecture is pleasing and distinguishable from less masterly works in a manner that it is hard to understand; the essential nature of Poetry it is universally acknowledged to be almost impossible to define, and lastly the sense of <u>beauty</u> or of melancholy arising from a simple succession of sounds, that is to say an air or melody, is equally inexplicable.

But this feeling belongs to the <u>perception</u>, not the <u>reason</u> and is far below the level of a somewhat analogous but feebler feeling produced by the contemplation of wonderful and beautiful facts of science or knowledge in general, or those fixed principles and enduring convictions & emotions which form religion and all our sense of love and duty.

I have occupied so much space in considering this abstract subject, because this feeling it is, which proves the high position really held by music and which naturally suggests itself as a means of classification that is to say as the characteristic of the class in which music falls. We may define it conveniently by the somewhat comprehensive term of <u>Perceptive Pleasure</u> meaning any emotion, usually an agreeable one, produced by subjects of nature or art through the medium of the senses or mind but without the necessary exercise of the higher faculties of reason. Now it will be remembered that I have spoken and I believe with truth, of a large number & variety of objects or circumstances capable of producing perceptive pleasures. I enumerate them all and place them in one grand class, because the relation of each to the mind and its faculties are throughout of much the same nature or <u>order</u>, but they naturally fall into subclasses according to the <u>sense</u> or means through which they act on the mind. Music evidently belongs exclusively to the sense of hearing. The Exterior of nature and artificial works of beauty and grandeur, as well as their artificial representations by pictures, sculpture etc., act principally on the eye in the sense of sight, but these as well as music it must certainly be allowed, are more or less connected with the third and highest division of perceptive objects, viz. poetical ideas or mental pictures of beauty, and though even these may not quite comprise the origin of every form of what I have called perceptive enjoyment, the remainder are but insignificant in proportion & closely dependent on these.

All these objects and subjects which occur to me are fully represented in the diagram on the following page, under their respective subclasses.

The central & main division is that of Poetical Ideas which are however so closely connected with & derived from Natural Objects that the latter are placed along side in corresponding order in a column of their own but under the heading of Sight. In parallel order likewise on either side are the artificial representations of these ideas and objects by both sight & hearing, in the columns respectively of Art & Music and we have thus exhibited to us both the close connection yet evident distinction of all these sources of perceptive pleasure.

Notes

1 Jevons and economics

1 Previously published as Mosselmans, Bert and Michael V. White (2001) General Introduction, in: *Collected Economic Writings of W. S. Jevons*, 9 Volumes. London: Palgrave/Macmillan, pp. v–xxv. Reproduced with permission of Palgrave Macmillan.

2 Most of the biographical information is derived from Könekamp (1962, 1972), the daughter of Jevons' eldest son. Other shorter biographical surveys include Keynes (1936: 109–12), Schabas (1990: 12–30), Peart (1996a: 1–4), Black (1987), Alvey (1982: 351–3) and H. W. Jevons (1934). Much biographical information can also be derived from Jevons' published diary and letters [seven volumes edited by R. D. C. Black, see Black (1982) for more information on these volumes]. His wife Harriet A. Jevons edited a volume with extracts from his journal and letters, which was published in 1886. The work of Harriet A. Jevons after Jevons' death is investigated by Könekamp (1982).

3 See Jevons' letters from 19 July 1856 (Black 1973: 235–7), 10 February 1857 (Black 1973: 262–8) and 7 April 1857 (Black 1973: 282–7).

4 Jevons' period in Manchester has been investigated by Chaloner (1972). Black (1993: 171–9) provides much information on Jevons' activities as a teacher in Manchester.

5 A result of this bibliographical work is Jevons' impressive (partly annotated) bibliography of logic, to be found in the John Rylands University Library of Manchester (JA6/5/11–220).

6 During the 1864–5 session, Jevons held a 'small professorship' in logic, mental and moral philosophy at Queen's College, Liverpool. He combined this activity with his tutorship in Manchester. See Black (1993: 173–4) for more details.

7 Black (1993: 182) continues by arguing that Jevons should be seen as a transitional figure not only in both economic theory and policy (see below), but also in the process of the institutionalization of economics at British universities. He was trained outside the ancient universities, but had a career as a teacher of political economy in the new university colleges.

8 Jevons' explorations in economic methodology, statistics and probability are in close accordance with his contributions to logic and philosophy of science. See Chapter 4 for a discussion of Jevons' 'extent in meaning in logic and economics'.

9 See Morgan (1990: 21–6) for a discussion of the reactions of some of Jevons' contemporaries.

10 It is clear that these activities would be harmful for the capitalists as well, but a struggle for higher wages would be injurious to the economy as a whole and to the labouring class in particular. It is clear that *The State in Relation to Labour* is written from a social and moral point of view, and it does not choose sides in the struggle between

capitalists and labourers – rather, it denies the existence of this struggle. Everybody should receive his proper share of the produce, but the labour should take place in acceptable conditions. Insurance activities and improvements in safety are socially and morally acceptable, whereas actions devoted to an artificial increase in certain wages are not.

2 Jevons and the history of economic thought

11 Previously published as Mosselmans, B. (2000a) Cracking the Canon: William Stanley Jevons and the Deconstruction of 'Ricardo', in: Psalidopoulos, M. (ed.) *The Canon in the History of Economics: Critical Essays*. London: Routledge, pp. 127–45.

12 Hammond's Editorial, as well as some comments, are available at http://www.cica. es/ehnet/Archives/hes/ may-97/.

13 The influence of Lardner's *Railway Economy* on Jevons has been investigated by some scholars. White (1982) stresses the influences of Pell, Woolley and Whately and refutes the *primordial* influence of Lardner; Hutchison (1982) re-emphasizes the influence of Lardner, on which he receives a response by White (1984); Hutchison's (1984) rejoinder summarizes both views, as he acknowledges that both Lardner and Pell are important; Bostaph (1989a,b) finally tries to reinforce Hutchison's opinion concerning Lardner's central influence, and stresses the importance of Bulwer-Lytton's *My Novel*.

14 See the previous footnote for some references on Woolley's lecture and Bulwer-Lytton's novel.

15 He does not mention Ricardo's *Principles*, which suggests that he knew Ricardo through the eyes of Mill, at least until 1858.

3 Jevons and statistics

16 Previously published as Mosselmans, B. (2005a) 'Adolphe Quetelet, the Average Man and the Development of Economic Methodology', *European Journal of the History of Economic Thought* 12(4), Winter 2005.

17 It is not my intention to give an exhaustive biography. More information is provided by Lottin (1912: 1–103).

18 See Wellens-De Donder (1966) for an exhaustive index of Quetelet's correspondence.

19 See Freund (1977) for a discussion of Comte versus Quetelet. Porter (1986: 41) argues that Quetelet 'pirated' Comte's concept of 'physique sociale', although he departed radically from positivism.

20 This first main work is in fact a collection of earlier published papers and studies.

21 Although not mentioned explicitly, Quetelet may have had the growing tendency towards free trade in mind. Quetelet was a proponent of free trade and attended the free trade conference (*Congrès des Economistes*) in 1847.

22 See Cooper and Murphy (2000) for Quetelet's reliance on aesthetic notions when constructing the 'average man'.

23 In his *Letters*, Quetelet elaborates on causes, distinguishing constant, variable and accidental causes. Constant causes act in a continuous manner, with the same intensity and the same direction. Variable causes act also in a continuous way, but with changing intensity and with changing tendencies (e.g. periodicity in seasons). Accidental causes act only fortuitously in any possible direction (Quetelet 1846: 157–60). Here and elsewhere, it is clear that Quetelet is inspired by meteorology, another scientific discipline to which he contributed thoroughly.

24 Porter (1986: 45) argues that Quetelet proclaimed the universality of the rule of numbers, '*Mundum regunt numeri*'. However, Quetelet's discussion of the measurement of intelligence remains largely unsuccessful. He discusses examination results and the

influence of age on intellectual development, and makes some superficial references to the intermixture of physical, moral and intellectual faculties of man (Quetelet 1848: 114–42).

25 It is clear that this statement does not remove, but incorporates the contradiction. Particularity is defined here as being universal. Many philosophers will not like this statement, to say the least. Here, Quetelet is inspired by Victor Cousin, who was influenced by Hegel. Only 'great individuals' would be able to change the world sensibly, and those 'great individuals' are inspired by the 'hidden spirit' of their age. This explains why precisely 'average' individuals are most suitable for this task (see Lottin 1912).

26 See also Armatte and Droesbeke (1997). The authors hold that Quetelet is therefore co-responsible for 'le dogme de la loi normale' that dominated the second half of the nineteenth century.

27 See also Desrosières (1993). MacKenzie (1981: 9) argues that Quetelet had but little direct impact on the development of statistics in Britain. However, Goldman (1991) argues that Quetelet was a 'catalyst' for the British statistical movement. In particular, three ideas were important: the regularity of social phenomena was demonstrable by the use of statistical analysis; even in the 'moral realm', there were regularities 'of the order of physical facts'; and these regularities stemmed from social conditions rather than from aggregated individual wills. These developments were important for the establishment of a 'predictive science of society which could rationally explain human behaviour in the aggregate'.

28 'La moyenne statistique est repatriée dans l'univers de l'individualisme méthodologique, et le "type collectif" n'est plus assimilé au "type moyen"' (my translation).

29 But also historical science: Buckle (1858) was inspired by Quetelet when he wrote his *History of Civilization in England*.

30 Michael White comments that Jevons not only read Quetelet directly, but also discussions that appeared in the *Sydney Magazine of Science and Art* and Herschel's review article.

31 Schabas (1990: 18, 161, note 44) recognizes that Quetelet's influence on Jevons was important. She argues that Jevons borrowed his ideas about average (individuals) and the fictitious mean from Quetelet, but that he failed to acknowledge the source, and therefore he probably forgot about Quetelet. Although this would be compatible with Jevons' odd idea about Quetelet being a German, he does refer to the *Letters on Probability*, in which Quetelet's ideas about real and arithmetical averages are explained more systematically than in the *Treatise on Man*.

32 Obviously, other influences on Jevons can be identified as well. Bentham, another major influence on Jevons, used the term 'body' to denote an aggregation of individuals, and White (2001) discusses the origin of this concept from within the natural sciences. These discussions would lead us too far – this paper merely argues that the identification of aggregate and average was taken from Quetelet.

33 White (1989b) shows that Jevons regarded the 'laws of supply and demand' as an empirical matter. Each law expresses a specific relationship between a (group of) consumer(s) and a good.

34 White (1994b: 434) acknowledges that Jevons was influenced by Quetelet's argument that human behaviour was normally distributed. White (1994a) investigates the influence of Richard Jennings on Jevons' representation of behaviour in mechanical and functional form.

35 'Wir müssen uns vielmehr an zusammengehörige Menschengruppen halten, welche, wie die Bevölkerung einer Stadt, einer Provinz, eines Staates, wie eine ganze Nation ein *organisch zusammengehörendes Ganze* bilden, das durch zahllose Fäden materieller, geistiger und gemüthlicher Beziehungen unter sich verknüpft ist, und so aus homogenen Bestandtheilen besteht' (my translation).

36 'Finding laws is therefore possible as such, without learning more about the inner

nature of the causes' (Wagner 1864: 66). ('Die Auffindung von Gesetzen ist daher auch an sich denkbar, ohne dass dadurch über das innere Wesen der Ursachen ein weiterer Aufschluss gewonnen wird', my translation.) The stability in the propensity to crime is an example of a regularity: the accidental causes cancel each other out, and the fundamental (material, spiritual, moral and economic) causes remained unchanged (Wagner 1864: 77). The relevant causes therefore include economic, spiritual and moral relations (or *institutions*). Wagner's adoption of the 'average man' has been criticized in a review, signed 'B.', and published in the *Jahrbücher* in 1865. The reviewer objects to Wagner's use of the concept of statistical 'laws' and argues that they should rather be seen as features of specific groups of individuals, expressed in numbers. He also objects to the idea of 'propensities', as this expresses the statement that something of the aggregate must be contained in the individual. This is an elaborate criticism of the 'average man'. The 'average man' is just an average, and it is unclear where he comes from and what he signifies, and the propensity (*Impuls*) is just a construction of the mind and nothing real (B 1965: 291). Statistical regularities are not laws, as this would require that we derive the laws from collective individual behaviour (i.e. 'wie fangen es die Kreidewesen an, um den Kreidekreis zu bilden?') (B 1865: 292). But, even if it is taken for granted that the 'average man' makes sense, then the question arises how many observations must be made. Simply taking the average leads to a stable number, even if no general or common causes are present. There is also no guarantee that individual causes will cancel each other out.

37 Knapp (1871) is an extensive review of Quetelet's writings that prepared his 1872 appraisal of Quetelet as a theoretician.

38 For more information about Jevons and measurement, see Maas (2001).

4 Jevons and logic

39 Previously published as Mosselmans, B. (1998a) 'William Stanley Jevons and the Extent of Meaning in Logic and Economics', *History and Philosophy of Logic* 19: 83–99. This article received the 'History of Economic Analysis Award' from the European Society for the History of Economic Thought, 2000/2001.

40 George Croom Robertson (1842–92) was Professor of Logic and Mental Philosophy at University College London, and editor of *Mind*. His criticism of Jevons' logic appeared in the first volume of *Mind* (Black 1977b: 239).

41 Frege's solution to the problem is clearly described by Russell (1946: 784). An instance of 'number' is a particular number such as '3', and an instance of '3' is a particular triad. The triad is a plurality; the number '3' is a plurality of pluralities; and 'number' in general is a plurality of pluralities of pluralities. The concept of 'number' is no longer identified with 'plurality', as in Jevons.

42 Edgeworth argues that Jevons' two equations are only one equation, namely:

$$\frac{\phi_1(a-x)}{\psi_1 y} = \frac{\phi_1 x}{\psi_1(a-y)}$$

as the only condition that has to be fulfilled for the two variables x and y (Edgeworth 1881: 20–1).

43 Keynes (1930: 71–8) criticized Jevons' procedure to 'average out' data round a 'mean' in the context of index numbers: 'What is the flaw in the argument? In the first place it is assumed that the fluctuations of individual prices round the "mean" are "random" in the sense required by the theory of the combination of independent observations. In this theory the divergence of one "observation" from the true position is assumed to have no influence on the divergences of other "observations". But in the case of prices a movement in the price of one commodity necessarily influences the movement in

the prices of other commodities, whilst the magnitudes of these compensatory movements depend on the magnitude of the change in expenditure on the first commodity
as compared with the importance of the expenditure on the commodities secondarily
affected. Thus, instead of "independence", there is between the "errors" in the successive "observations" what some writers on probability have called "connexity", or, as
Lexis expressed it, there is "sub-normal dispersion".' This criticism can be extended
to Jevons' conception of a 'trading body'. See also Peart (1996a: 211).

5 Jevons and institutions

44 Previously published as Mosselmans, B. (2003) 'The Role of Institutions in Jevons's
Economics', *History of Economic Ideas* X/2002/3: 47–60.
45 For an overview of 'old' institutionalism, see Oser (1963: 330–5) or Hodgson
(1993).
46 Hodgson emphasizes that the concept 'market' should only be used in cases when
we can really speak about *institutionalized* mechanisms. Becker's use of a marriage
market or Doeringer and Piore's description of internal labour markets within firms
do not fulfil this condition because, in both cases, no institutionalized processes of
buying and selling can be detected.
47 Moreover, the question of a reduction in working hours does not belong to the domain
of economic theory as such, because a 'higher calculus' of pleasures and pains is
needed. This discussion should include considerations about the family of the labourer, whereas the pure theory contains individuals with an exclusive attention towards
their own interests (White 1994b: 439–40).
48 We repeat that Jevons' ideas regarding the achievement of a general equilibrium
theory appear to be incomplete from today's point of view. It is of course possible to
link Jevons' conception of human capital theory with the determination of labour supply, but he did not treat this subject in depth. It is clear that he hinted in that direction,
but he did not systematically develop the consequences of his scattered remarks on
this subject.

6 Jevons and religion

49 Previously published as Mosselmans, B. and G. D. Chryssides (2005) 'Unitarianism
and Evolutionism in W. S. Jevons' Thought', *Faith and Freedom* 58(1), Spring and
Summer, No. 160: 18–44.
50 See Robinson (1981) for a discussion of Channing's influence on the development
of Unitarian theology. Holt (1938: 342) illustrates Channing's influence in England:
in 1842, nearly 3000 people subscribed to a cheap edition of his works and, in 1869,
about 21,000 copies of another edition were sold in twelve months.
51 The liberal middle class was not 'some simple and unified world of ideas predicated
on political economy and utilitarian philosophy'. The liberal bloc contained different
and opposed constituents. The hostility towards Unitarians rose together with their
growing political power. In 1851, there were about 1670 Manchester Unitarians at
worship on census day (Seed 1982: 11; Wach 1993: 542–3).
52 As American Unitarianism played an important role in the American literary renais-
sance, literary scientists are inclined to restrict Unitarianism to a literary movement.
Unitarians welcomed art and literature as aids in the transmission of doctrines, but not
art and literature nor the doctrines as such were primordial objectives; Unitarians were
interested foremost in raising ethical consciousness.
53 The 'newer' congregations, established since the middle of the nineteenth century,
became stronger missionary movements that wanted to spread their faith among the
working class. The 'older' congregations consisted mainly of wealthy and better educated Unitarians who were less willing to support these missionary activities. These

people preferred to present themselves as an unsectarian group that did not have a creed (Holt 1938: 339).

54 Holt (1938: 169) states: 'Under the pseudonym of Gamaliel he (Bentham) wrote a book with the characteristic title *Jesus not Paul*. He shared the idea long popular among Unitarians that it was St. Paul who corrupted Christianity from its original simplicity. The idea is, of course, based not so much on St. Paul's own writings as on their use by later theologians.'

55 William Jevons junior produced several writings on religion, including *Systematic Morality* (1829) and *The Claims of Christianity to the Character of the Divine Relation Considered* (1870). It is likely that Stanley sent comments on the latter work to his uncle (Black 1977c: 11). There was some correspondence between Stanley and William junior but, unfortunately, the volumes edited by Black contain only the letters from William junior to Stanley. It is therefore not possible to examine Stanley's opinion of his uncle's writings, nor to investigate how William junior's writings influenced the development of Stanley's religious beliefs.

56 For a similar statement, see Black (1973: 395). This illustrates Jevons' view that all religions refer to the same body of moral truths, but use different costumes according to their state of civilization (or character). For Jevons' use of 'character' and 'race', see White (1994a,b).

57 Ian Steedman comments that Gladstone was a prominent Anglican, so Jevons may have attempted to minimize their theological differences.

58 Readers of Wittgenstein's *Tractatus* will doubtless see the similarity with his proposition 6.44: 'Not *how* the world is, is the mystical, but *that* it is.'

59 We should keep in mind that Jevons argued that 'induction is really the inverse process of deduction' (Jevons 1874: 12), which implies that he should have had no problems with this approach.

60 This idea could possibly explain why Unitarians embraced Spencer's evolutionary thought, as it is compatible with the disappearance of external authority.

61 In the letter, he writes: 'When I read the *First Principles* I was occasionally puzzled to know exactly in what sense he spoke of the persistence of force' (Black 1977b: 29). This sounds like a statement about a book that he read several years ago.

62 See Jevons (1879a: 535–8), Black (1977d: 24). In the same letter to Mills (see above), Jevons writes: 'I daresay that a great many of the details and illustrations of Spencer's philosophy will not stand examination, and I think it is a pity that he has attempted to produce a complete system of philosophy' (Black 1977b: 29). Jevons is certainly no unconditional follower of Spencer's doctrines: in *The State in Relation to Labour*, he subscribes to Spencer's ideas regarding the division of labour (Jevons 1882: 44–5) but, in *Money and the Mechanism of Exchange*, he condemns Spencer for overlooking Gresham's law (Jevons 1875: 64, 82; Black 1995a: 190).

63 It is a rather short section, but *The Principles of Science* is about the methodology of science, not about scientific theories themselves. Jevons (1874: 762) is clearly an adherent of evolutionary theory: 'I question whether any scientific works which have appeared since the *Principia* of Newton are comparable in importance with those of Darwin and Spencer, revolutionising as they do all our views of the origin of bodily, mental, moral and social phenomena'.

64 In the first edition of the *Principles*, Jevons refers to William Thomson's argument that we cannot 'trace the heat-history of the Universe to an infinite distance in the past'. This implies that there was either some initial distribution of heat that did not emerge from a previous distribution, or some discontinuity of natural law (Jevons 1874: 744). Clifford objects that Jevons is generalizing the laws of conduction of heat towards laws of nature. In the Preface to the second edition of the *Principles*, Jevons admits that 'the known laws of nature do not enable us to assign a "beginning"'. But he also refers to the natural scientists Tait and Maxwell to conclude that 'the theory

of heat indicates the occurrence of some event of which our science cannot give any further explanation' (Jevons 1874: xxxii).

65 R. D. C. Black adds that Jevons gave up teaching in and after 1880 and therefore had much more free time. While this may explain an increase in output, it does not explain why Jevons precisely opted for writings on social and ethical questions.

66 See the bibliography composed by Inoue and White (1993). Black (1995a: 189) recognizes that Spencer becomes more important to Jevons after 1867, but he wonders why there is no earlier reference to Spencer, although Jevons must have been well acquainted with Spencer's writing before this. Although this is a conjecture that cannot be proved because of insufficient historical evidence, it may be due to his reading of *First Principles*, which may have occurred slightly before 1867. His increased interest in social questions after 1879 may then have been influenced by his reading of *The Data of Ethics*.

67 See also Peart (1996b: 137–69) for more on Jevons' use of utilitarianism and for the statement that his policy proposals are very similar to Mill's proposals.

68 White comments that this is only the case for proposed policies that cannot be directly assessed in terms of their effects on the accumulation of wealth. For instance, free trade is always beneficial as protectionism interferes 'with the natural tendency of exchange to increase utility' (Jevons 1911: 142–6; White 1994b). No 'higher calculus' is therefore required in this specific case.

69 Despite some indirect economic effects, mechanical economics is insufficient to discuss this policy issue. Establishing public libraries is not justified because they would increase labour productivity. The 'higher calculus' has to be brought in because the effects are realized through a change in moral habits and thus in character.

7 Jevons and music

70 Previously published as Mosselmans, B. and E. Mathijs (1999a) 'Jevons's Music Manuscript and the Political Economy of Music', *History of Political Economy*, Vol. 31, Supplement 'Economic Engagements with Art', pp. 121–56.

71 This paper contains hitherto unpublished material by Jevons (see Appendix), which was found in the Jevons' archives at the John Rylands Library of the Manchester University. Parts of the archives ('On the Functions of Music', JA6/47/8 and a diagram, JA6/45/4) are reproduced by courtesy of the Director and University Librarian, the John Rylands University Library of Manchester. We would like to thank Peter Nockles for his kind help with the archives, and John Vint and the Manchester Metropolitan University for the support during my stay in Manchester. This paper is part of the OZR project 1971131490 financed by the Research Council of the Free University of Brussels. We received many interesting comments at and after the conference, and we would like to thank Neil De Marchi, Craufurd Goodwin, Judy Klein, Harro Maas and Michael V. White for their specific remarks. Michael White's comments were especially useful, as he directed our attention to several aspects of Jevons' context and to some additional archive material. All remaining errors are, of course, ours.

72 Michael White urged us not to neglect other important contextual aspects. Indeed, Jevons did not start his reflections on 'selfishness' after the death of his father, as earlier remarks in his journal indicate (Black and Könekamp 1972: 112; White 1989a: 624). Woolley's lecture on 'The Selfish Theory of Morals' should be seen as a major influence, as it enabled Jevons to couch his analysis of 'selfishness' in terms of pleasures and pains (Black and Könekamp 1972: 132–4; White 1982: 337–8, 1989a: 625). This lecture therefore crystallized Jevons' thoughts on this subject. On the other hand, whereas Jevons visits the lecture in September 1856, he receives the news of his father's death in February of the same year. We agree with White that the lecture provided Jevons with more analytical rigour, but the death of his father gave

his reflections a more personal and existential dimension. This becomes clear from a review of Jevons' letters to his sister Henrietta, which are filled with matters of a more intimate nature.

73 This is, once again, not to neglect other influences. See the previous footnote for the argument that Woolley's lecture supplied Jevons' reflections with more analytical rigour. For the discussion of Jevons' early influences, see La Nauze (1941), Hutchison (1982, 1984), White (1982, 1984, 1989a), Bostaph and Shieh (1986), Bostaph (1989a,b).

74 This is in accordance with White's description of Jevons' 'naturalistic theory of ethics': 'what was good or ethical could be characterized in terms of "sensible" properties of the world and hence could be discussed and identified in empirically meaningful terms' (White 1994b: 431).

75 According to White, Jevons made some misleading statements regarding his solitude, and he tended to exaggerate his intellectual isolation. See for example Jevons' activities as a photographer (Burke 1955). His numerous articles for newspapers (Inoue and White 1993) indicate that Jevons did not live in intellectual isolation. We argue, however, that Jevons' solitude remains important with regard to his ideas on music (and religion) (see below).

76 In an article for *The Sydney Morning Herald*, published on 7 October 1858, Jevons makes clear that the character of a city is connected with the character of its inhabitants. Jevons describes the 'Rocks' as a dirty and unhealthy part of Sydney, inhabited by immoral and drunken people. Here, the complete absence of sanitation should be condemned. Proper sanitation may be a step in the direction of the elevation of the morality of the masses (Jevons 1858). For the role of music in the process of civilization, see section four.

77 We would like to thank Michael V. White for drawing our attention to the music material in the Henrietta section. We analyse it at the end of the next section.

78 White notes that the chapter 'On the Functions of Music' was to follow the chapter 'On Musical Rhythm and Time', and that Jevons intended to add at least one chapter that would appear in between these two chapters. As there is no trace of this chapter, it may be possible that it was never written. See White (1996: 2).

79 See Harro Maas' contribution to this conference: 'Invention, Economic Man, and the Factory System'.

80 This observation gives a new dimension to Klein's (1995: 136) remark that Jevons had low qualities of visualization. He responded to a query by Francis Galton that he had severe difficulties in forming geometric conceptions in his mind. This low visualization capability may partly explain why Jevons seems not to be interested at all in other art forms than music. His detailed descriptions of musical pieces contrast heavily with other very superficial descriptions of art, such as his visit to the Louvre: 'It is a magnificent palace filled with all sorts of collections of pictures, sculpture antiquities, etc., etc., but the most celebrated I believe are the pictures by the old painters' (Black 1973: 58). He writes about an exhibition of paintings in London that 'there were of course a great many fine paintings, but also a great many foolish and absurd ones, and a very large number of portraits which are very dull' (Black 1973: 76). As the contrast with his descriptions of music is indeed very striking, we may conclude that, although Jevons had a low capability for visualization when it comes to graphics, he had a very high capability for visualization of music. And this may (at least partly) explain his interest in music and his disinterest in other forms of art.

81 Jevons refers in this manuscript to a chapter on 'musical harmony', which indicates that it is in fact a part of the 'On the science and art of music' project. Moreover, the reference is to an unnumbered chapter, whereas the chapter on harmony in the 'science and art' manuscript is marked as Chapter two. This suggests that the writings to be found in the Henrietta section are earlier because, otherwise, Jevons would probably have referred to Chapter two. This manuscript elaborates on the division of the

arts (where the chapter reproduced in the Appendix stops) and on Jevons' criticism on Alison's *Essays on Taste*. We return to both issues later.

82 For a concise treatment of Shaftesbury's connection with Locke, see Marsh (1961).

83 Jevons' utilitarian treatment of art is similar to Bentham's fragmentary remarks on the subject. Bentham states that art is a source of pleasure which should be used for a moral elevation of the masses. He even argues that art may be a good substitute for drunkenness (Bentham 1825). These ideas appear in Jevons' policy prescriptions as well (see next section).

84 Charles Corkran, a Unitarian minister, remarks in a letter to Jevons that he agrees with Jevons' suggestions, but he states that concerts in London are difficult for reasons of climate and distance. He already proposed a similar policy to 'a very active Broad Church vicar', but the proposal fell through (Black 1977b: 292).

85 See White (1993) and White (1994b) for Jevons' use of the category 'race' and White (1994c) for Jevons' use of the category 'gender'.

86 Elsewhere, we elaborate on the general problem in Jevons' thought that he is unable to link conceptions of individuals with conceptions of aggregates of individuals (Mosselmans 1998a).

Bibliography

Primary sources: Jevons Archives, John Rylands University Library, University of Manchester. For a complete list of these sources, see McNiven (1983).

Adamson, R. [1881] (1988) 'Review of W. S. Jevons' Studies in Deductive Logic', *Mind* 6: 427–33, reprinted in: Wood, J. C. (ed.) *William Stanley Jevons: Critical Assessments*, Vol. I. London: Routledge, 30–36.

Aerts, D., E. Mathijs and B. Mosselmans (eds) (1999) *Science and Art: The Red Book of Einstein Meets Magritte*. Dordrecht: Kluwer.

Aldrich, J. (1987) 'Jevons as Statistician: The Role of Probability', *Manchester School of Economics and Social Studies* 55(3): 233–56.

—— (2000) 'The Jevonian Revolution in International Trade Theory', *Journal of the History of Economic Thought* 22(1): 65–84.

Alison, A. [1790] (1968) *Essays on the Nature and Principles of Taste*. Hildesheim: Olms.

Alvey, J. (1982) 'Stanley Jevons: A Centennial Assessment', *Economic Analysis and Policy* 12(2): 35–50, reprinted in: Wood, J. C. (ed.) *William Stanley Jevons: Critical Assessments*, Vol. I. London: Routledge, 351–68.

—— (1986) 'Review of Papers and Correspondence of William Stanley Jevons, Volumes I–VII, 1972–1981', *History of Economic Thought Society of Australia Newsletter* 6: 53–5.

Anderson, J. L. (1967) 'Ricardo on Rent: A Comment', *Australian Economic History Review* 7: 217–19.

Anonymous [1871] (1988) 'Review of *The Theory of Political Economy*', *Saturday Review* 11: 624–5, reprinted in: Wood, J. C. (ed.) *William Stanley Jevons: Critical Assessments*, Vol. II. London: Routledge, 5–10.

Armatte, M. and J.-J. Droesbeke (1997) 'Quetelet et les probabilités: le sens de la formule', in: *Actualité et universalité de la pensée scientifique d'Adolphe Quetelet*. Brussel: Académie Royale de Belgique, 107–35.

B. (1965) 'Die Gesetzmässigkeit in den scheinbar willkürlichen menschlichen Handlungen vom Standpunkte der Statistik. Von Dr. Adolph Wagner. Hamburg, Boyes und Geisler, 1864.' *Jahrbücher für Nationalökonomie und Statistik* 4: 286–301.

Backhouse, R. [1985] (1987) *A History of Modern Economic Analysis*. Oxford: Basil Blackwell.

Bagehot, W. (1875) 'A New Standard of Value', *The Economist*, November 20, reprinted in: *Economic Journal*, vol. 2 (1892).

Baldwin, J. M. [1901] (1925) 'Logical Machines', in: Baldwin, J. M. (ed.) *Dictionary of Philosophy and Psychology*, Vol. III. New York: Macmillan, 28–30, reprinted in: *Modern Logic*, Vol. 7, no. 1, January 1997, pp. 78–80.

Bartier, J. (1977) 'Quetelet politique', in: *Adolphe Quetelet 1796–1874. Mémorial Adolphe Quetelet No. 4*. Brussel: Palais des Académies, 20–45.

Bentham, J. [1789] (1996) *An Introduction to the Principles of Morals and Legislation*. Oxford: Clarendon Press.

—— [1825] (1998) 'Reward Applied to Art and Science', in: Harrison, P., C. Wood and J. Gaiger (eds) *Art in Theory (1815–1900)*. Oxford: Blackwell, 149–51.

Birch, A. (1967) *The Economic History of the British Iron and Steel Industry 1784–1879*. London: Frank Cass.

Birken, L. 1988) 'From Macroeconomics to Microeconomics: the Marginalist Revolution in Sociocultural Perspective', *History of Political Economy* 20(2): 251–64.

Black, R. D. C. (1960) 'Jevons and Cairnes', *Economica* 27(107): 214–32.

—— (1962) 'W.S. Jevons and the Economists of His Time', *Manchester School of Economics and Social Studies* 30(3): 203–21.

—— (1970) 'Introduction', in: Jevons, W.S. *The Theory of Political Economy*. Harmondsworth: Penguin Books, 7–40.

—— (1972a) 'Jevons, Bentham and De Morgan', *Economica* 39(153): 119–34.

—— (1972b) 'Jevons, Marginalism and Manchester', *The Manchester School* 40(1): 2–8.

—— (1972c) 'W. S. Jevons and the Foundation of Modern Economics', *History of Political Economy* 4(2): 364–78.

—— (ed.) (1973) *Papers and Correspondence of William Stanley Jevons, Volume II. Correspondence 1850–1862*. London: Macmillan.

—— (ed.) (1977a) *Papers and Correspondence of William Stanley Jevons, Volume VI. Lectures on Political Economy 1875–1876*. London: Macmillan.

—— (ed.) (1977b) *Papers and Correspondence of William Stanley Jevons, Volume IV. Correspondence 1873–1878*. London: Macmillan.

—— (ed.) (1977c) *Papers and Correspondence of William Stanley Jevons, Volume III. Correspondence 1863–1872*. London: Macmillan.

—— (ed.) (1977d) *Papers and Correspondence of William Stanley Jevons, Volume V. Correspondence 1879–1882*. London: Macmillan.

—— (ed.) (1981) *Papers and Correspondence of William Stanley Jevons, Volume VII. Papers on Political Economy*. London: Macmillan.

—— (1982) 'The Papers and Correspondence of William Stanley Jevons: A Supplementary Note', *The Manchester School* 50(4): 417–28.

—— (1987) 'Jevons, William Stanley (1835–1882)', in: Eatwell, J. *et al.* (eds) *The New Palgrave*, Vol. 2. London: Macmillan, 1008–14.

—— (1990) 'Jevons, Marshall and the Utilitarian Tradition', *Scottish Journal of Political Economy* 37(1): 5–17.

—— (1992) 'Attempts by Jevons and Walras to Publicise Each Other's Work', *Revue Européenne des sciences sociales* 30(92): 109–29.

—— (1993) 'Jevons' Contribution to the Teaching of Political Economy in Manchester and London', in: Kaish, A. and K. Tribe (eds) *The Market for Political Economy*. London: Routledge, 162–83.

—— (1995a) 'Transitions in Political Economy II: Economic Policy', in: *Economic Theory and Policy in Context*. Aldershot: Edgar Elgar, 181–201.

—— (1995b) 'Transitions in Political Economy I: Economic Analysis', in: *Economic Theory and Policy in Context*. Aldershot: Edgar Elgar, 163–80.

Black, R. D. C. and R. Könekamp (eds) (1972) *Papers and Correspondence of William Stanley Jevons, Volume I. Biography and Personal Journal*. London: Macmillan.

Blaug, M. [1962] (1997) *Economic Theory in Retrospect*. Cambridge: Cambridge University Press.

—— (1972) 'Was There a Marginal Revolution?' *History of Political Economy* 4(2): 269–80.

Böhm-Bawerk, E. [1884] (1959) *Capital and Interest*. South-Holland (Illinois): Libertarian Press, 3 vols.

Bostaph, S. (1989a) 'Jevons' "Antipodean Influence": the Question of Early Influences', *History of Political Economy* 21(4): 601–23.

—— (1989b) 'Response', *History of Political Economy* 21(4): 631–3.

Bostaph, S. and Y.-N. Shieh. (1986) 'W. S. Jevons and Lardner's Railway Economy', *History of Political Economy* 18(1): 49–64.

—— (1987) 'Jevons' Demand Curve', *History of Political Economy* 19(1): 107–26.

Boulding, K. E. (1971) 'After Samuelson, Who Needs Adam Smith?', *History of Political Economy* 3(2): 225–37.

Bourdieu, P. [1979] (1984) *Distinction*. London: Routledge.

—— (1994) 'The Link between Artistic and Literary Struggles', in: Colhier, P. and R. Lethbridge (eds) *Artistic Relations*. New Haven, CT: Yale University Press, 30–9.

Bowley, M. (1972) 'The Predecessors of Jevons – the Revolution that Wasn't', *The Manchester School* 40(1): 9–29.

Bowman, R. S. (1989) 'Jevons' Economic Theory in Relation to Social Change and Public Policy', *Journal of Economic Issues* 23(4): 1123–47.

—— (1997a) 'The Place of Education in W. S. Jevons' Political Economy', *The European Journal of the History of Economic Thought* 4(3): 455–77.

—— (1997b) 'Policy Implications of W. S. Jevons' Economic Theory', *Journal of the History of Economic Thought* 19: 196–221.

Brahmananda, P. R. (1971) 'Jevons' Theory of Political Economy – A Centenary Appraisal', *Indian Economic Journal* 19(2): 128–42.

Brems, Hans (1987) 'Dansk okonomisk teori efter 1870: var Svenskerne bedre?' [Danish economic theory after 1870: were the Swedes better?], *Nationalokonomisk Tidsskrift* 125(2): 244–52.

Briggs, A. (1973) 'Review of Papers and Correspondence of William Stanley Jevons, Volumes I and II', *Economic Journal* 83: 1010–12.

Broome, J. (1991) 'Utility', *Economics and Philosophy* 7(1): 1–12.

Brown, H. G. [1931] (1988) 'Opportunity Cost: Marshall's Criticism of Jevons', *American Economic Review* 21(3): 498–500, reprinted in: Wood, J. C. (ed.) *William Stanley Jevons: Critical Assessments*, Vol. II. London: Routledge, 109–11.

Brownlie, A. D. and M. F. Lloyd-Prichard (1963) 'Professor Fleemin Jenkin, 1833–1885, Pioneer in Engineering and Political Economy', *Oxford Economic Papers* 15(3): 204–16.

Buckle, H. (1858) *History of Civilization in England*, Vol. I. London: John W. Parker.

Buehrens, J. A. and Forrest Church [1989] (1998) *A Chosen Faith. An Introduction to Unitarian Universalism*. Boston: Beacon Press.

Burke, I. [1955] (1988) 'Australia's First Pictorialist', *Australian Photo Review* 62: 6–22, reprinted in: Wood, J. C. (ed.) *William Stanley Jevons: Critical Assessments*, Vol. I. London: Routledge, 188–96.

Cairnes, J. E. [1872] (1988) 'New Theories in Political Economy', *Fortnightly Review*,

New Series 11: 71–6, reprinted in: Wood, J. C. (ed.) *William Stanley Jevons: Critical Assessments*, Vol. II. London: Routledge, 11–16.

Chaloner, W. H. (1972) 'Jevons in Manchester: 1863–1876', *The Manchester School* 40(1): 73–84.

Chamberlin, E. H. [1932] (1969) *The Theory of Monopolistic Competition. A Re-orientation of the Theory of Value*. Cambridge, MA: Harvard University Press.

Chandler, L. V. [1948] (1953) *The Economics of Money and Banking*. New York: Harper & Brothers.

Channing, W. E. [1819] 'Unitarian Christianity', Lecture delivered at the Ordination of Rev. Jared Sparks in The First Independent Church of Baltimore on 5 May 1819 [http://xroads.virginia.edu/~HYPER/DETOC/religion/unitarian.html].

Checkland, S. G. [1951] (1988) 'Economic Opinion in England as Jevons Found It', *Manchester School of Economic and Social Studies* 19(1): 143–69, reprinted in: Wood, J. C. (ed.) *William Stanley Jevons: Critical Assessments*, Vol. I. London: Routledge, 125–45.

Chryssides, George D. (1998) *The Elements of Unitarianism*. Shaftesbury: Element.

Clark, J. B. (1891) 'Distribution as Determined by a Law of Rent', *The Quarterly Journal of Economics* 5: 289–318.

—— [1899] (1908) *The Distribution of Wealth. A Theory of Wages, Interest and Profits*. London: Macmillan.

Clovis [1964–5] (1988) 'Jevons and the Establishment', *American Scholar* 34(1): 109–11, reprinted in: Wood, J. C. (ed.) *William Stanley Jevons: Critical Assessments*, Vol. III. London: Routledge, 82–5.

Comim, F. V. (1998) '"Jevons And Menger Re-Homogenized? Jaffe After 20 Years": A Comment on Peart', *American Journal of Economics and Sociology* 57(3): 341–4.

Cooper, B. P. and M. S. Murphy (2000) 'The Death of the Author at the Birth of Social Science: the Cases of Harriet Martineau and Adolphe Quetelet', *Studies in the History and Philosophy of Science* 31(1): 1–36.

Coser, L. A. (1971) *Masters of Sociological Thought. Ideas in Historical and Social Context*. New York: Harcourt Brace Jovanovich.

Crafts, N. F. R. and T. C. Mills (1994) 'Trends in Real Wages in Britain, 1750–1913', *Explorations in Economic History* 31: 176–94.

Creedy, John (1986) 'On the King–Davenant "Law" of Demand', *Scottish Journal of Political Economy* 33(3): 193–212.

Davanzati, G. F. (1995) 'W. S. Jevons: from the Wage Fund Doctrine to the Theory of Individual Supply of Labour', *History of Economic Ideas* III/1995/2: 33–50.

Darwin, G. H. [1875] (1988) 'The Theory of Exchange Value', *Fortnightly Review*, New Series 17: 243–53, reprinted in: Wood, J. C. (ed.) *William Stanley Jevons: Critical Assessments*, Vol. II. London: Routledge, 89–99.

Davison, G. (1997–98) 'The Unsociable Sociologist: W. S. Jevons and his Survey of Sydney, 1856–8', *Australian Cultural History* 16: 127–50.

Deane, P. (1989) *The State and the Economic System. An Introduction to the History of Political Economy*. Oxford: Oxford University Press.

De Marchi, N. B. (1973) 'The Noxious Influence of Authority: A Correction of Jevons' Charge', *Journal of Law and Economics* 16(1): 179–89.

Descartes, R. [1637] (1991) *Discours de la méthode*. Saint-Amand: Editions Gallimard.

Desrosières, A. (1993) *La politique des grands nombres*. Paris: La Découverte.

—— (1997) 'Quetelet et la sociologie quantitative: du piédestal à l'oubli', in: *Actualité et universalité de la pensée scientifique d'Adolphe Quetelet.* Brussel: Académie Royale de Belgique, 179–98.

Devi, S. U. (1972) 'Comments on Prof. Brahmananda's Article on Jevons' Theory of Political Economy – A Centennial Appraisal', *Indian Economic Journal* 20(2): 294–9.

Dobb, M. (1973) *Theories of Value and Distribution Since Adam Smith. Ideology and Economic Theory.* London: Cambridge University Press.

Donoghue, Mark (1997) 'Fleeming Jenkin and the Wage Fund Debates, 1866–1871: A Neglected Contribution', *History of Economic Ideas* 5(1): 87–105.

Edgeworth, F. Y. [1881] (1967) *Mathematical Psychics. An Essay on the Application of Mathematics to the Moral Sciences.* New York: Augustus M. Kelley.

Ekelund, R. B. (1976) 'A Short-Run Classical Model of Capital and Wages: Mill's Recantation of the Wages Fund', *Oxford Economic Papers* 28(1): 66–85.

Ekelund, R. B. and Y.-N. Shieh (1989) 'Jevons on Utility, Exchange, and Demand Theory: A Reassessment', *The Manchester School* 57(1): 17–33.

Fayazmanesh, S. (1998) 'The Magical, Mystical "Paradox of Value"', *Research in the History of Economic Thought and Methodology* 16: 123–53.

Fieser, J. (1993) 'Moore, Spencer, and the Naturalistic Fallacy', *History of Philosophy Quarterly* 10: 271–7.

Fine, B. (1990) *The Coal Question. Political Economy and Industrial Change from the Nineteenth Century to the Present Day.* London: Routledge.

Fischer, N. (1979) *Economy and Self. Philosophy and Economics from the Mercantilists to Marx.* Westport, CT: Greenwood Press.

FitzPatrick, P. J. (1960) 'Leading British statisticians of the nineteenth century', *Journal of the American Statistical Association* 55: 38–70.

—— (1977) 'Leading British statisticians of the nineteenth century' in: Kendall, M. G. and R. L. Plackett (eds) *Studies in the History of Statistics and Probability II.* London: Griffin, 180–212.

Fontaine, P. (1998) 'Menger, Jevons, and Walras Un-Homogenized, De-Homogenized, and Homogenized: A Comment on Peart', *American Journal of Economics and Sociology* 57(3): 333–40.

Frantzen, P. [1973] (1986) *Overzicht van het economisch denken. Een Marxistische analyse.* Antwerp: Kluwer.

Frege, G. [1884] (1968) *Die Grundlagen der Arithmetik [The Foundations of Arithmetic.]* Oxford: Basil Blackwell.

Freund, J. (1977) 'Quetelet et Auguste Comte', in: *Adolphe Quetelet 1796–1874. Mémorial Adolphe Quetelet No. 4.* Brussel: Palais des Académies, 46–64.

Gallegati, M. (1994) 'Jevons, Sunspot Theory and Economic Fluctuations', *History of Economic Ideas* 2(2): 23–40.

Garcia-Mata, C. and F. I. Schaffner [1934] (1988) 'Solar and Economic Relationships: A Preliminary Report', *Quarterly Journal of Economics* 49: 1–51, reprinted in: Wood, J. C. (ed.) *William Stanley Jevons: Critical Assessments,* Vol. III. London: Routledge, 15–54.

Giocoli, N. (1998) 'The "True" Hypothesis of Daniel Bernoulli: What Did the Marginalists Really Know?', *History of Economic Ideas* 6(2): 7–43.

Goldman, L. (1991) 'Statistics and the Science of Society in Early Victorian Britain. An Intellectual Context for the General Register Office', *Social History of Medicine* 4(3): 415–34.

Gomes, A. W. [1955] (1998) *Unitarian Universalism.* Grand Rapids, MI: Zondervan Publishing House.

Grattan-Guinness, I. (1988) 'Living Together and Living Apart. On the Interactions between Mathematics and Logics from the French Revolution to the First World War', *South African Journal of Philosophy* 7(2): 73–82.

—— (1991) 'The Correspondence between George Boole and Stanley Jevons, 1863–1864', *History and Philosophy of Logic* 12: 15–35.

Grindhammer, L. W. (1975) *Art and the Public: The Democratization of the Fine Arts in the United States 1830–1860*. Tübingen: Metzler.

Groenewegen, P. (1995) *A Soaring Eagle: Alfred Marshall 1842–1924*. Aldershot: Edward Elgar.

Halbwachs, M. (1913) *La théorie de l'homme moyen. Essai sur Quetelet et la statistique morale*. Paris: Félix Alcan.

Halsted, G. B. [1878] (1988) 'Professor Jevons' Criticism of Boole's Logical System', *Mind* 3: 134–7, reprinted in: Wood, J. C. (ed.) *William Stanley Jevons: Critical Assessments*, Vol. I. London: Routledge, 26–9.

Hammond, J. D. (1997) 'Taxonomy in History of Economics', HES Mailing List Editorial, May 1997 [http://www.cica.es/ehnet/Archives/hes/may-97].

Harrison, Charles and Paul Woods (eds) [1992] (1993) *Art in Theory 1900 1990. An Anthology of Changing Ideas*. Oxford: Blackwell Publishers, 123–213.

Harley, R. (1883) 'Obituary of William Stanley Jevons', *Proceedings of the Royal Statistical Society* 35: 1–12.

Hart, H. L. A. (1996) 'Bentham's Principle of Utility and the Theory of Penal Law', in: Bentham, J. [1789] (1996) *An Introduction to the Principles of Morals and Legislation*. Oxford: Clarendon Press, lxxix–cxii.

Hébert, R. F. (1998) 'Jevons and Menger Re-Homogenized: Who is the Real "Odd Man Out"? A Comment on Peart', *American Journal of Economics and Sociology* 57(3): 327–32.

Heertje, A. (1982) 'An Important Letter from W. S. Jevons to L. Walras', *The Manchester School* 50(4): 412–16.

Heimann, E. [1945] (1964) *History of Economic Doctrines*. New York: Oxford University Press.

Held, A. (1867) 'Adam Smith und Quetelet', *Jahrbücher für Nationalökonomie und Statistik* 9: 249–79.

Hempel, C. G. and P. Oppenheim [1948] (1953) 'The Logic of Explanation', in: Feigl, Herbert and May Brodbeck (eds) *Readings in the Philosophy of Science*. New York: Appleton-Century-Crofts, 319–52.

Henderson, J. P. (1992) 'Astronomy, Astrology, and Business Cycles: Hyde Clarke's Contribution', *Research in the History of Economic Thought and Methodology* 9: 1–34.

Henderson, P. (1997) *Early Mathematical Economics. William Whewell and the British Case*. Lanham: Rowman & Littlefield.

Hennings, K. H. (1979) 'George Darwin, Jevons, and the Rate of Interest', *History of Political Economy* 11(2): 199–212.

Herford, C.H. (1931) *Philip Wicksteed, His Life and Work*. London: J. M. Dent.

Herschel, T. (1835) 'On Man, and the Development of his Faculties', *The Athenaeum*, 8 August 1835: 593–4; 15 August 1835: 611–13; 29 August 1835: 658–61 [http://www.stat.ucla.edu/history/athenaeum.pdf].

Higgins, B. H. [1935] (1988) 'W. S. Jevons – A Centenary Estimate', *Manchester School of Economic and Social Studies* 6: 103–11, reprinted in: Wood, J. C. (ed.) *William Stanley Jevons: Critical Assessments*, Vol. I. London: Routledge, 50–8.

Hobsbawm, E. J. [1968] (1984) *Industry and Empire. From 1750 to the Present Day*. Harmondsworth: Penguin.

Hobson, J. A. (1891) 'The Law of the Three Rents', *The Quarterly Journal of Economics* 5: 263–88.

Hodgson, G. (1988) *Economics and Institutions. A Manifesto for a Modern Institutional Economics*. Cambridge: Polity Press.

—— (1993) 'Institutional Economics: Surveying the "Old" and the "New"', *Metroeconomica* 44(1): 1–28.

—— (1998) 'The Approach of Institutional Economics', *Journal of Economic Literature* 36(1): 166–92.

Holt, R. V. (1938) *The Unitarian Contribution to Social Progress in England*. London: George Allen & Unwin Ltd.

Horvath, R. A. (1977) 'Quetelet et Marx. Essai de synthèse de leurs pensées au point de vue statistique et sociologique', in: *Adolphe Quetelet 1796–1874. Mémorial Adolphe Quetelet No. 4*. Brussel: Palais des Académies, 87–99.

Howe, C. A. (1997) *For Faith and Freedom. A Short History of Unitarianism in Europe*. Boston: Skinner House Books.

Howe, D. W. (1970) *The Unitarian Conscience. Harvard Moral Philosophy, 1805–1861*. Cambridge, MA: Harvard University Press.

Howey, R. S. (1972) 'The Origins of Marginalism', *History of Political Economy* 4(2): 269–80.

Hutchison, T. [1953] (1966) *A Review of Economic Doctrines 1870–1929*. Oxford: Clarendon Press.

—— (1969) 'Economists and Economic Policy in Britain after 1870', *History of Political Economy* 1(2): 231–55.

—— (1978) *On Revolutions and Progress in Economic Knowledge*. Cambridge: Cambridge University Press.

—— (1982) 'The Politics and Philosophy in Jevons' Political Economy', *The Manchester School* 50(4): 366–78.

—— (1984) 'Mr. White on Jevons: A Rejoinder', *The Manchester School* 52(1): 73–4.

—— (1994a) 'White on "the Irish Factor" in Jevons' Statistics: a Rebuttal', *History of Economics Review* 21: 65–70.

—— (1994b) 'Three Strikes Against White', *History of Economics Review* 21: 87.

Inoue, T. (1986a) 'Bibliographical List of W. Stanley Jevons' Writings, etc., including the Reviews and the Translations of his Writings, and Obituaries on him', *The Journal of Economics of Kwansei University* 39(4), January.

—— (1986b) 'Index of Correspondence between W. S. Jevons and His Correspondents', *The Journal of Economics of Kwansei University* 40(3), October.

Inoue, T. and M. V. White (1993) 'Bibliography of Published Works by W. S. Jevons', *Journal of the History of Economic Thought* 15: 122–47, updated and reprinted in Jevons (2001) *Collected Economic Writings*, Vol. 1. London: Palgrave/Macmillan.

Jaffé, W. (1976) 'Menger, Jevons and Walras De-Homogenized', *Economic Inquiry* 14(4): 511–24.

Jenkins, K. (1991) *Re-thinking History*. London: Routledge.

Jevons, H. A. (ed.) (1886) *Letters and Journal of William Stanley Jevons*. London: Macmillan.

Jevons, H. S. [1934] (1988) 'William Stanley Jevons: His Scientific Contributions', *Econometrica* 2: 231–7, reprinted in: Wood, J. C. (ed.) *William Stanley Jevons: Critical Assessments*, Vol. I. London: Routledge, 44–9.

Jevons, H. W. [1934] (1988) 'William Stanley Jevons: His Life', *Econometrica* 2: 225–31, reprinted in: Wood, J. C. (ed.) *William Stanley Jevons: Critical Assessments*, Vol. I. London: Routledge, 37–43.

Jevons, T. E. [1889] (1988) 'Mr. Wicksteed's Notes upon Jevons', *Quarterly Journal of Economics* 3: 500–3, reprinted in: Wood, J. C. (ed.) *William Stanley Jevons: Critical Assessments*, Vol. II. London: Routledge, 46–8.

Jevons, W. S. [1858] The Social Cesspools of Sydney No. 1 – The Rocks. *The Sydney Morning Herald*, 7 October 1858, typescript provided by Michael V. White.

—— (1863a) 'On the Study of Periodic Commercial Fluctuations', in: *Report of the British Association for the Advancement of Science*, Cambridge, 157–8.

—— (1863b) 'Notice of a General Mathematical Theory of Political Economy', in: *Report of the British Association for the Advancement of Science*, Cambridge, 158–9.

—— [1865, 1906] (1965) *The Coal Question*. New York: Augustus M. Kelley.

—— [1866] (1965) 'Brief Account of a General Mathematical Theory of Political Economy', in: *The Theory of Political Economy*. New York: Augustus M. Kelley, 303–14.

—— [1869, 1890] (1991) 'The Substitution of Similars', in: *Pure Logic and Other Minor Works*. Bristol: Thoemmes.

—— (1871) *The Theory of Political Economy*, First Edition. London: Macmillan and Co.

—— [1874] (1879) *The Principles of Science: A Treatise on Logic and Scientific Method*. London: Macmillan.

—— (1875) *Money and the Mechanism of Exchange*. London: Kegan Paul, Trench, Trübner & Co.

—— [1878] (2001) *Science Primers. Political Economy*. Writings on Economics, Vol. 5, Palgrave Archive Edition. London: Macmillan.

—— [1879a, 1957] (1965) *The Theory of Political Economy*, Fifth Edition. New York: Augustus M. Kelley.

—— (1879b) 'John Stuart Mill's Philosophy Tested. IV – Utilitarianism', *Contemporary Review* 36: 521–38.

—— [1882, 1910] (1968) The State in Relation to Labour. London: Macmillan.

—— [1883] (1965) *Methods of Social Reform*. New York: Augustus M. Kelley.

—— [1884] (1909) *Investigations in Currency and Finance*. London: Macmillan.

—— [1905] (1965) *The Principles of Economics*. New York: Augustus M. Kelley.

—— [1911] (2001) *The Theory of Political Economy*, Fourth Edition, London: Macmillan.

—— (2001) *Collected Economic Writings*, 9 volumes. London: Palgrave/Macmillan.

—— (2002) *Reviews and Obituaries*, 2 volumes, with a general introduction by Takatoshi Inoue and headnotes by Bert Mosselmans. Bristol: Thoemmes Press.

Kallich, M. (1948) 'The Meaning of Archibald Alison's Essays on Taste', *Philological Quarterly* 27: 314–24.

Kenton, R. (1971) 'Hours at Work: Jevons' Labor Theory after 100 Years', *Industrial Relations* 10(2): 227–30.

Kenworthy, F. (1966) 'From Authority to Freedom in Church Life. The Act of Uniformity and Unitarian Dissent', *Transactions of the Unitarian Historical Society* 12(4): 141–54.

Keynes, J. M. [1912] (1988) 'Review of W. S. Jevons' Theory of Political Economy', *Economic Journal* 22: 78–80, reprinted in: Wood, J. C. (ed.) *William Stanley Jevons: Critical Assessments*, Vol. II. London: Routledge, 49–50.

—— [1930] (1971) *A Treatise on Money. The Collected Writings of John Maynard Keynes*, Volume V. London: Macmillan.

—— [1936] (1972) 'William Stanley Jevons', in: *Essays in Biography. The Collected Writings of John Maynard Keynes*, Vol. X. London: Macmillan, 109–60.

Kim, J. (1997) 'Newmarch, Cairnes and Jevons on the Gold Question and Statistics', *Journal of the History of Economic Thought* 19: 49–70.

Klein, J. (1995) 'The Method of Diagrams and the Black Arts of Inductive Economics', in: Rima, I. H. (ed.) *Measurement, Quantification and Economic Analysis*. London: Routledge, 98–139.

—— (1997) *Statistical Visions in Time. A History of Time Series Analysis 1662–1938*. Cambridge: Cambridge University Press.

Knapp, G. F. (1871) 'Bericht über die Schriften Quetelets zur Sozialstatistik und Anthropologie', *Jahrbücher für Nationalökonomie und Statistik* 17: 167–74, 342–58, 427–45.

—— (1872) 'A. Quetelet als Theoretiker', *Jahrbücher für Nationalökonomie und Statistik* 18: 89–124.

Kneale, W. and M. Kneale.[1962] (1968) *The Development of Logic*. Oxford: Clarendon Press.

Könekamp, R. (1962) 'William Stanley Jevons (1835–1882). Some Biographical Notes', *Manchester School of Economics and Social Studies* 30(3): 251–73.

—— (1972) 'Biographical Introduction', in: Black, R. D. C. and R. Könekamp (eds) *Papers and Correspondence of William Stanley Jevons*, Vol. I. London: Macmillan, 1–52.

—— (1982) 'The Work of Harriet Ann Jevons (1838–1910) after Her Husband's Death', *The Manchester School* 50(4): 379–411.

Kriesler, P. [1984] (1988) 'On Dobb's Interpretation of Jevons on Ricardo', *Cambridge Journal of Economics* 8(4): 294–7.

Laidler, D. (1982) 'Jevons on Money', *The Manchester School* 50(4): 326–53.

—— (1988) 'British Monetary Orthodoxy in the 1870s', *Oxford Economic Papers* 40(1): 74–109.

Landreth, H. and D. Colander (1994) *History of Economic Thought*. Boston: Houghton Mifflin.

Langlois, R. N. (1986a) 'The New Institutional Economics: an Introductory Essay', in: Langlois, R. N. (ed.) *Economics as a Process. Essays in the New Institutional Economics*. Cambridge: Cambridge University Press, 1–25.

—— (1986b) 'Rationality, Institutions and Explanation', in: Langlois, R. N. (ed.) *Economics as a Process. Essays in the New Institutional Economics*. Cambridge: Cambridge University Press, 225–55.

La Nauze, J.A. [1941] (1988) 'Jevons in Sydney', *Economic Record* 17:31–45, reprinted in: Wood, J. C. (ed.) *William Stanley Jevons: Critical Assessments*, Vol. I. London: Routledge, 109–24.

—— [1953] (1988) 'The Conception of Jevons' Utility Theory', *Economica* 20: 356–8, reprinted in: Wood, J. C. (ed.) *William Stanley Jevons: Critical Assessments*, Vol. III. London: Routledge, 58–60.

Leslie, T. E. C. [1879] (1988) 'Untitled Review of the Second Edition', *The Academy* 377: 59–60, reprinted in: Wood, J. C. (ed.) *William Stanley Jevons: Critical Assessments*, Vol. II. London: Routledge, 23–7.

Logan, B. and Y.-N. Shieh (1990) 'Westergaard, Jevons and an Early Contribution to Constrained Optimization', *Manchester School of Economics and Social Studies* 58(1): 20–31.

Lottin, J. (1912) *Quetelet. Statisticien et sociologue*. Leuven: Institut Supérieur de Philosophie & Félix Alcan.

Lynch, P. (1973) 'Review of Papers and Correspondence of William Stanley Jevons, Volumes I and II', *Economic and Social Review* 5(1): 147–50.

Maas, H. (1999a) 'Pacifying the Workman: Ruskin and Jevons on Labor and Popular Culture', in: De Marchi, N. and C. D. W. Goodwin (eds) 'Economic Engagements with Art', *History of Political Economy* (Supplement): 85–120.

—— (1999b) 'Mechanical Rationality: Jevons and the Making of Economic Man', *Studies in History and Philosophy of Science* 30(4): 587–619.

—— (2001) *Mechanical Reasoning: Jevons and the Making of Modern Economics*. Amsterdam: Proefschrift Universiteit van Amsterdam.

Maas, H. and B. Mosselmans (2002) 'William Stanley Jevons (1835–1882)', in: *Dictionary of 19th-Century British Philosophers*. Bristol: Thoemmes Press, 598–604.

Machlup, F. (1964) 'Professor Samuelson on Theory and Realism', *American Economic Review* 54: 733–6.

MacKenzie, D. A. (1981) *Statistics in Britain 1865–1930. The Social Construction of Scientific Knowledge*. Edinburgh: Edinburgh University Press.

MacLennan, B. (1972) 'Jevons' Philosophy of Science', *The Manchester School* 40(1): 53–71.

McNiven, P. (1983) 'Hand-List of the Jevons Archive in the John Rylands University Library', *Bulletin of the John Rylands University Library* 66: 213–55.

Malthus, T. R. [1798] (1986) *An Essay on the Principle of Population: First Edition. The Works of Thomas Robert Malthus*, Volume One. London: William Pickering.

—— [1826] (1986) *An Essay on the Principle of Population: Sixth Edition. The Works of Thomas Robert Malthus*, Volumes Two and Three. London: William Pickering.

Marsh, R. (1961) 'Shaftesbury's Theory of Poetry: the Importance of "Inward Colloquy"', *English Literary History* 28: 54–69.

Marshall, A. [1872] (1988) 'Mr Jevons' Theory of Political Economy', *The Academy* 1 April 1872: 141–6, reprinted in: Wood, J. C. (ed.) *William Stanley Jevons: Critical Assessments*, Vol. II. London: Routledge, 17–22.

—— [1874] 'A Note', published anonymously in 'Notes and News', *The Academy* 6: 558 (21 November 1874), reprinted in: *Marshall Studies Bulletin* 4 (1994): 1–17.

—— [1890, 1920] (1966) *Principles of Economics*. London: Macmillan.

Martineau, J. [1890] (1898) *The Seat of Authority in Religion*. London: Longmans, Green & Co.

Martins, R. (1998) 'Jevons e o papel da analogia na arte da descoberta experimental: o caso da descoberta dos raios X e sua investigação pré-teórica' [Jevons and the role of analogy in the art of experimental discovery: the case of the discovery of X rays and their pre-theoretical investigation]. *Episteme. Filosofia e História das Ciências em Revista* 3(6): 222–49.

Mathijs, E. and B. Mosselmans (1997) 'Van herbelevende waarheid naar afgebeelde schoonheid: de versluiering van het oorspronkelijk geweld bij Plato en Aristoteles', in: Pijnenburg, L. (ed.) *Vijandbeelden in de filosofie*. Wageningen: Landbouwuniversiteit, 67–71.

—— (1998) 'Van Daedalus tot Pygmalion: Kunst en mimesis in het antropometrische stadium', *Tijdschrift voor Filosofie* 60(3): 521–53.

—— (1999) 'Art and Science in a Fragmented World: Einstein meets Magritte as a Forum for Communication', in: Aerts, D., E. Mathijs and B. Mosselmans (eds) *Einstein Meets Magritte. The Red Book: Science and Art*. Dordrecht: Kluwer, xvii–xxiii.

—— (2000a) 'Mimesis and the Representation of Reality: a Historical World View', *Foundations of Science* 5(1): 61–102.

—— (2000b) 'Mimesis als fundamenteel motief in fictionele representaties', in: Mathijs, E. and W. Hessels (eds) *Waarheid en werkelijkheid. Feitelijke, fictionele en artistieke representaties van de realiteit.* Brussel: VUB Press, 97–116.

Mays, W. (1962) 'Jevons' Conception of Scientific Method', *Manchester School of Economics and Social Studies* 30(3): 223–49.

Mays, W. and D. P. Henry [1952] (1988) 'Exhibition of the Work of W. Stanley Jevons', *Nature* 170: 696–7, reprinted in: Wood, J. C. (ed.) *William Stanley Jevons: Critical Assessments*, Vol. III. London: Routledge, 55–7.

—— [1953] (1988) 'Jevons and Logic', *Mind* 62: 484–505, reprinted in: Wood, J. C. (ed.) *William Stanley Jevons: Critical Assessments*, Vol. I. London: Routledge, 167–87.

Mazlish, B. (1986) 'Jevons' Science and his "Second Nature"', *Journal of the History of Behavioural Sciences* 22: 140–9.

Michotte, P. (1904) *Etudes sur les théories économiques qui dominèrent en Belgique de 1830 à 1886.* Leuven: Charles Peeters.

Mill, J. S. [1848, 1909] (1973) *Principles of Political Economy with Some of Their Applications to Social Philosophy.* Clifton, NJ: Augustus M. Kelley.

—— [1871] (1904) *Principles of Political Economy with Some of Their Applications to Social Philosophy.* London: Longmans, Green & Co.

Mineka, F. E. (1944) The Dissidence of Dissent. The Monthly Repository, 1806–1838. Doctoral dissertation, Chapel Hill: The University of North Carolina Press.

Mirowski, P. (1984) 'Macro Economic Instability and the "Natural" Processes in Early Neoclassical Economics', *Journal of Economic History* 44(2): 345–54.

—— (1989) *More Heat than Light. Economics as Social Physics: Physics as Nature's Economics.* Cambridge: Cambridge University Press.

Mises, L. [1949] (1996) *Human Action.* Irvington: Foundation for Economic Education.

Moore, J. R. (1979) *The Post-Darwinian Controversies. A Study of the Protestant Struggle to Come to Terms with Darwin in Great Britain and America.* Cambridge: Cambridge University Press.

Morgan, M. S. [1990] (1995) *The History of Econometric Ideas.* Cambridge: Cambridge University Press.

Mosselmans, B. (1992) De relevantie van de hedendaagse wetenschapsfilosofische theorieën in het kader van de ekonomische wetenschap. Een kritische analyse, Eindverhandeling VUB (MA Thesis), Brussel: VUB.

—— (1993) 'De Popper-Kuhn kontroverse in de ekonomische wetenschap', in: Van Dooren, W. and T. Hoff (eds) *Aktueel filosoferen.* Delft: Eburon, 28–32.

—— (1994a) De relevantie van enkele recente wetenschapsfilosofische theorieën in het kader van de ekonomische wetenschap. Een historisch-kritische analyse, Eindverhandeling VUB (MA Thesis), Brussel: VUB.

—— (1994b) 'Laudan, Barnes en Giere: een oplossing voor de Popper-Kuhn kontroverse in de ekonomische wetenschap?' in: Van Bendegem, J. P. and G. C. Cornelis (eds) *Iedereen die niet denkt zoals ik, volge mij.* Brussel: VUB Press, 68–73.

—— (1995a) Enkele historisch-methodologische studies omtrent de geschiedenis van het economisch denken. Voorbereidend werk, doctorale opleiding, Brussel: VUB.

—— (1995b) 'De fundering van de neo-klassieke economie: een (grond)slag in de lucht?', in: Ter Hark, M., P. S. Hasper and R. G. Hilbrands (eds) *Congresbundel Filosofiedag,* Groningen 1995, 64–7.

—— (1996a) 'Historiografie, ideeëngeschiedenis en de geschiedenis van het economisch denken', De Uil van Minerva. *Tijdschrift voor Geschiedenis en Wijsbegeerte van de Cultuur* 12(4): 223–35.

—— (1996b) 'Een kritische bespreking van het neo-classicisme volgens Daniel M. Hausman: introspectie en cirkelfundering', *Nieuw Tijdschrift van de VUB* 9(2): 122–37.

—— (1996c) 'William Stanley Jevons (1835–1882): logicus, econoom, en voorloper van het logisch empirisme', in: Groot, G., H. Oosterling and W. Prins (eds) *Van agora tot markt*. Rotterdam: Erasmus Universiteit, 305–10.

—— (1997a) 'De normatieve wetenschapsfilosofie in het kader van de economische wetenschap', *Nieuw Tijdschrift van de VUB* 10(1): 41–56.

—— (1997b) 'De weggelaten wiskunde van Hans von Mangoldt', *Economisch Statistische Berichten* 82(4115): 592–4.

—— (1998a) 'William Stanley Jevons and the Extent of Meaning in Logic and Economics', *History and Philosophy of Logic* 19: 83–99.

—— (1998b) 'Jevons on Measurement: a Comment', *Recherches Economiques de Louvain* 64(3): 347–51.

—— (1998c) 'Reproduction and Scarcity: Hidden Agenda of the Marginal Revolution', *History of Economics Society Monthly Guest Editorial*, April 1998 [http://www.eh.net/ HisEcSoc/ Resources/Editorials/Mosselmans/].

—— (1999a) 'Reproduction and Scarcity: the Population Mechanism in Classicism and in the "Jevonian Revolution"', *The European Journal of the History of Economic Thought* 6(1): 34–57.

—— (1999b) 'Economie en ethiek: het verhaal van een moeizame boedelscheiding', *Mores. Pedagogisch Tijdschrift voor Morele Problemen* 44(217): 121–30.

—— (1999c) 'Bentham, Jevons en de introductie van de "nutscalculus" in de politieke economie', *Tijdschrift voor Politieke Economie* 22(1): 59–72.

—— (1999d) 'De Methodenstreit in de 19de-eeuwse Economische Wetenschap', in: Baars, Jan and Richard Starmans (eds) *Het eigene en het andere: Filosofie en Globalisering*. Delft: Eburon, 227–33.

—— (1999e) From Classical to Neoclassical: the Economic Thought of William Stanley Jevons (1835–1882) and its Relation to his Ethics, Logic and Aesthetics. Doctoral Dissertation, Brussel: VUB.

—— (2000a) 'Cracking the Canon: William Stanley Jevons and the Deconstruction of "Ricardo"', in: Psalidopoulos, M. (ed.) *The Canon in the History of Economics: Critical Essays*. London: Routledge, 127–45.

—— (2000b) 'The Omitted Mathematics of Hans von Mangoldt', *Journal of Economic Studies* 27(4/5): 382–93.

—— (2000c) 'William Stanley Jevons (1835–1882)', in: Powell, J., D. W. Blakeley and T. Powell (eds) *Makers of Western Culture 1800–1914*. Westport CT: Greenwood Press, 222–23.

—— (ed.) (2001a) *Kunst te koop? Over bruggen en breuken tussen kunst en economie*. Roeselare: Roularta.

—— (2001b) 'Bibliography of Secondary Sources', in: *Collected Economic Writings of W. S. Jevons*, 9 volumes. London: Palgrave/Macmillan, xliv–liv.

—— (2001c) 'De economie van kunst en cultuur: contradictio in terminis?', in: Mosselmans, B. (ed.) *Kunst te koop? Over bruggen en breuken tussen kunst en economie*. Roeselare: Roularta, 43–62.

—— (2002) 'Commentary: Jevons, Marx, and Keynes – and the Political Economy of the Pub', *Journal of the History of Economic Thought* 24(2): 251–2.

—— (2003) 'The Role of Institutions in Jevons' Economics', *History of Economic Ideas* X/2002/3: 47–60.

—— (2005a) 'Adolphe Quetelet, the Average Man and the Development of Economic Methodology', *European Journal of the History of Economic Thought* 12(4): 565–82.

—— (2005b) 'Jevons, William Stanley', in: Beckert, J. and M. Zafirovski (eds) *Encyclopedia of Economic Sociology*. London: Routledge.

—— (2005c) 'Scarcity', in: Beckert, J. and M. Zafirovski (eds) *Encyclopedia of Economic Sociology*. London: Routledge.

—— (2005d) 'Utility', in: Beckert, J. and M. Zafirovski (eds) *Encyclopedia of Economic Sociology*. London: Routledge.

Mosselmans, B. and G. D. Chryssides (2005) 'Unitarianism and Evolutionism in W. S. Jevons' Thought', *Faith and Freedom* 58(Pt 1) 160: 18–44.

Mosselmans, B. and E. Mathijs (1997) 'Petrella in Wonderland? De Groep van Lissabon en het rijk van de schaarste', *Streven. Cultureel Maatschappelijk Maandblad* 64(10): 914–22.

—— (1998a) 'René Girard, het zondebokmechanisme en het denken van Aristoteles', *De Uil van Minerva. Tijdschrift voor Geschiedenis en Wijsbegeerte van de Cultuur* 14(3): 179–94.

—— (1998b) 'Natuurlijke ongelijkheid en hiërarchische differentiatie in de antropometrische wetenschappen van Aristoteles', in: Hoenen, Maarten J. F. M. and M. Schijvenaars (eds) *Metamorphose*. Acten 20ste Nederlands-Vlaamse Filosofiedag. Nijmegen: Katholieke Universiteit, 299–306.

—— (1999a) 'Jevons' Music Manuscript and the Political Economy of Music', *History of Political Economy* 31(Supplement 'Economic Engagements with Art'): 121–56.

—— (1999b) 'Similarity or Difference: the Case for Interdisciplinarity in Natural Sciences, Social Sciences, and Art and Aesthetics', in: Aerts, D., E. Mathijs and B. Mosselmans (eds) *Einstein Meets Magritte. The Red Book: Science and Art*. Dordrecht: Kluwer, 11–20.

—— (2000) 'Human Culture and Science: Equality and Inequality as Foundations of Scientific Thought', *Foundations of Science* 5(3): 339–78.

—— (2002) 'Science and Philosophy in the Anthropometric Stage', in: Neuenschwander, E. and L. Bouquiaux (eds) *Science, Philosophy and Music. Proceedings of the XX. International Congress of History of Science*. Turnhout: Brepoels, 57–65.

Mosselmans, B. and M. V. White (2001) 'General Introduction', in: *Collected Economic Writings of W. S. Jevons*, 9 volumes. London: Palgrave/Macmillan, v–xxv.

Negishi, T. (1982) 'A Note on Jevons' Law of Indifference and Competitive Equilibrium', *Manchester School of Economics and Social Studies* 30(3): 220–30.

Neurath, O. (1970) 'Unified Science as Encyclopedic Integration', in: Neurath, Otto, Rudolf Carnap and Charles Morris (eds) *Foundations of the Unity of Science*, Vol. I. Chicago: The University of Chicago Press, 1–27.

—— (1983) *Philosophical Papers 1913–1946*. Dordrecht: Kluwer.

—— (1987) 'The New Encyclopedia', in: McGuinness, B. (ed.) *United Science*. Dordrecht: Kluwer, 132–41.

Noller, C. W. (1972) 'Jevons on Cost', *Southern Economic Journal* 39(1): 113–15.

Oser, J. (1963) *The Evolution of Economic Thought*. New York: Harcourt, Brace & World.

Paul, E. F. (1979) 'W. Stanley Jevons: Economic Revolutionary, Political Utilitarian', *Journal of the History of Ideas* 40: 267–83.

Peach, T. (1987) 'Jevons as an Economic Theorist', in: Eatwell, J. *et al.* (eds) *The New Palgrave*, Vol. 2. London: Macmillan, 1014–19.

Peart, S. (1990a) 'Jevons' Applications of Utilitarian Theory to Economic Policy', *Utilitas* 2(2): 281–306.

—— (1990b) 'The Population Mechanism in W. S. Jevons' Applied Economics', *The Manchester School* 58(1): 32–53.

—— (1991) 'Sunspots and Expectations: W. S. Jevons' Theory of Mood Fluctuations', *Journal of the History of Economic Thought* 13: 243–65.

—— (1993) 'W. S. Jevons' Methodology of Economics: Some Implications of the Procedures for "Inductive Quantification"' *History of Political Economy* 25(3): 435–60.

—— (1994) 'Jevons and the Population Mechanism: A Reply', *The Manchester School* 62(1): 103–8.

—— (1995) 'Disturbing Causes, Noxious Errors, and the Theory–Practice Distinction in the Economics of J. S. Mill and W. S. Jevons', *Canadian Journal of Economics* 27(4): 1195–211.

—— (1996a) *The Economics of William Stanley Jevons*. London: Routledge.

—— (1996b) 'Ignorant Speculation and Immoral Risks: Macheaths, Turpins and the Commercial Classes in Nineteenth-Century Theories of Economic Fluctuations', *The Manchester School* 64(2): 135–52.

—— (1998) 'Jevons and Menger Re-Homogenized? Jaffé after 20 Years', *American Journal of Economics and Sociology* 57(3): 307–25.

—— (2001) 'Facts Carefully Marshalled in the Empirical Studies of William Stanley Jevons', *History of Political Economy* 33(Special issue 'The Age of Economic Measurement'): 252–76.

Peel, J. D. Y. (1971) *Herbert Spencer. The Evolution of a Sociologist*. London: Heinemann.

Peirce, C. S. (1887) 'Logical Machines', *American Journal of Psychology* 1: 165–70, reprinted in: *Modern Logic* 7(1): 71–7, January 1997.

Porter, T. M. (1981) 'A Statistical Survey of Gases: Maxwell's Social Physics', *Historical Studies in the Physical and Biological Sciences* 12(1): 77–116.

—— (1985) 'The Mathematics of Society: Variation and Error in Quetelet's Statistics', *The British Journal of the History of Science* 18: 51–69.

—— (1986) *The Rise of Statistical Thinking: 1820–1900*. Princeton: Princeton University Press.

—— (1995) 'Statistical and Social Facts from Quetelet to Durkheim', *Sociological Perspectives* 38(1): 15–26.

Quetelet, A. [1835] (1991) *Sur l'homme et le développement de ses facultés, ou essai de physique sociale*. Paris: Bachelier.

—— (1836) *Sur l'homme et le développement de ses facultés, ou essai de physique sociale*. Brussel: Louis Hauman.

—— [1842] (1968) *A Treatise on Man and the Development of his Faculties*. New York: Burt Franklin.

—— (1846) *Lettres à S. A. R. Le Duc Régnant de Saxe-Cobourg et Gotha, sur la théorie des probabilités, appliquée aux sciences morales et politiques*. Brussel: M. Hayez.

—— (1848) *Du système social et des lois qui les régissent*. Paris: Guillaumin.

—— (1869) *Physique sociale ou Essai sur le développement des facultés de l'homme*. Brussel: Muquardt.

—— (1871) *Anthropométrie ou mesure des différentes facultés de l'homme*. Brussel: C. Muquardt.

—— (1873) *Congrès international de statistique*. Brussel: F. Hayez.

—— (1914) *Soziale Physik oder Abhandlung über die Entwicklung der Fähigkeiten des Menschen.* Jena: Gustav Fischer.

Reid, G. C. (1972) 'Jevons' Treatment of Dimensionality in "The Theory of Political Economy": An Essay in the History of Mathematical Economics', *The Manchester School* 40(1): 85–98.

Ricardo, D. [1810–11, 1951] (1966) 'Notes on Bentham', in: *Pamphlets and Papers 1809–1811. The Works and Correspondence of David Ricardo*, Vol. III. Cambridge: Cambridge University Press, 259–341.

—— [1816–1818] (1970) *The Works and Correspondence of David Ricardo, Vol. VII. Letters 1816–1818.* Cambridge: Cambridge University Press.

—— [1820] (1970) 'Funding System', in: *The Works and Correspondence of David Ricardo*, Vol. IV. Cambridge: Cambridge University Press, 143–200.

—— [1821] (1957) 'On the Principles of Political Economy and Taxation, 3rd edn', in: *The Works and Correspondence of David Ricardo*, Vol. I. Cambridge: Cambridge University Press.

—— [1821–23, 1951] (1966) 'Letters July 1821–1823', in: *The Works and Correspondence of David Ricardo*, Vol. IX. Cambridge: Cambridge University Press.

Robertson, G. [1876] (1988) 'Mr. Jevons' Formal Logic', *Mind* 1: 206–22, reprinted in: Wood, J. C. (ed.) *William Stanley Jevons: Critical Assessments*, Vol. 1. London: Routledge, 11–25.

Robertson, R. M. [1951] (1988) 'Jevons and his Precursors', *Econometrica* 19(3): 229–49, reprinted in: Wood, J. C. (ed.) *William Stanley Jevons: Critical Assessments*, Vol. I. London: Routledge, 146–66.

Robbins, L. [1936] (1982) 'The Place of Jevons in the History of Economic Thought', *The Manchester School* 50(4): 310–25.

Robine, M. (1990) 'La question charbonnière de William Stanley Jevons', *Revue Economique* 20(1): 56–61.

Robinson, D. (1981) 'The Legacy of Channing: Culture as a Religious Category in New England Thought', *Harvard Theological Review* 74(2): 221–39.

Rosen, F. (1996) 'Introduction', in: Bentham, J. [1789] (1996) *An Introduction to the Principles of Morals and Legislation*. Oxford: Clarendon Press, xxxi–lxix.

Russell, B. [1946] (1979) *History of Western Philosophy*. London: Unwin Paperbacks.

Russell, H.C. (1888) 'Astronomical and Meteorological Workers in New South Wales, 1778–1860', *Australasian Association for Advancement of Science* 1: 45–94.

Samuelson, P. (1963) 'Problems of Methodology – Discussion', *American Economic Review* 53: 231–6.

Schabas, M. (1984) 'The "Worldly Philosophy" of William Stanley Jevons', *Victorian Studies* 28(1): 129–47.

—— (1985) 'Some Reactions to Jevons' Mathematical Program: The Case of Cairnes and Mill', *History of Political Economy* 17(3): 337–53.

—— (1989) 'Alfred Marshall, W. Stanley Jevons, and the Mathematization of Economics', *Isis* 80(301): 60–73.

—— (1990) *A World Ruled by Number. William Stanley Jevons and the Rise of Mathematical Economics*. Princeton: Princeton University Press.

Schlee, E. E. (1992) 'Marshall, Jevons, and the Development of the Expected Utility Analysis', *History of Political Economy* 24: 729–44.

Schmitt, R. W. (1995) 'The Salt–Jinger Experiments of Jevons (1857) and Rayleigh (1880)', *Journal of Physical Oceanography* 25(1): 8–17.

132   Bibliography

Scholefield, H. B. (1954) 'The Building of a Free Church', in: Scholefield, H. B. (ed.) *A Pocket Guide to Unitarianism*. Boston: The Beacon Press, 31–42.

Schumpeter, J. A. [1954] (1967) *History of Economic Analysis*. London: George Allen & Unwin Ltd.

Seed, J. (1982) 'Unitarianism, Political Economy and the Antinomies of Liberal Culture in Manchester, 1830–1850', *Social History* 7(1): 1–25.

Shaftesbury, A. (1790) *Characteristics of Men, Manners, Opinions, Times with a Collection of Letters*. Basil: Tourneisen and Legrand.

Shaw, G. B. [1885] (1988) 'The Jevonian Criticism of Marx (A Comment on the Rev. P. H. Wicksteed's Article)', *Today: Monthly Magazine of Scientific Socialism*, New Series 3: 22–7, reprinted in: Wood, J. C. (ed.) *William Stanley Jevons: Critical Assessments*, Vol. II. London: Routledge, 100–5.

Sheehan, R. G. and R. Grieves (1982) 'Sunspots and Cycles: A Test of Causation', *Southern Economic Journal* 48(4): 775–7.

Smith, A. [1776] (1994) *An Inquiry into the Nature and Causes of the Wealth of Nations*. New York: The Modern Library.

Spencer, H. [1879] (1882) *The Data of Ethics*. New York: D. Appleton & Co.

—— (1898) *First Principles*, Fifth Edition, First Edition 1862. London: Williams & Northgate.

Steedman, I. (1972) 'Jevons' Theory of Capital and Interest', *The Manchester School* 40(1): 31–51.

—— (1986) 'Trade Interest & Class Interest', *Economia Politica* 3: 187–206, reprinted in: Steedman, I. (1989) *From Exploitation to Altruism*. Boulder, CO: Westview Press; Cambridge, UK: Polity Press in association with Blackwell.

—— (1997) 'Jevons' Theory of Political Economy and the "Marginalist Revolution"', *The European Journal for the History of Economic Thought* 4(1): 43–64.

Stigler, G. J. [1965] (1967) *Essays in the History of Economics*. London: The University of Chicago Press.

—— (1983) 'Review of Papers and Correspondence of William Stanley Jevons, Volume VII: Papers on Political Economy', *Economic Journal* 93: 415–7.

Stigler, S. M. (1986) *The History of Statistics. The Measurement of Uncertainty before 1900*. Cambridge, MA: Belknap Press of Harvard University Press.

—— (1982) 'Jevons as Statistician', *The Manchester School* 50(4): 354–65.

—— (1994) 'Jevons on the King–Davenant Law of Demand: A Simple Resolution of a Historical Puzzle', *History of Political Economy* 26(2): 185–91.

—— (1999) *Statistics on the Table. The History of Statistical Concepts and Methods*. Cambridge, MA: Harvard University Press.

Stolnitz, J. (1960) *Aesthetics and Philosophy of Art Criticism: a Critical Introduction*. Boston: Houghton Mifflin.

Strachey, A. [1878] (1988) 'J. S. Mill's Philosophy Tested by Prof. Jevons', *Mind* 3: 283–4, reprinted in: Wood, J. C. (ed.) *William Stanley Jevons: Critical Assessments*, Vol. III. London: Routledge, 9–10.

Strong, J. V. (1976) 'The Infinite Ballot Box of Nature: De Morgan, Boole and Jevons on Probability and the Logic of Induction', *Proceedings of the Philosophy of Science Association* 1: 197–211.

Uemiya, S. [1981] (1988) 'Jevons and Fleeming Jenkin', *Kobe University Economic Review* 27: 45–57, reprinted in: Wood, J. C. (ed.) *William Stanley Jevons: Critical Assessments*, Vol. III. London: Routledge, 174–88.

Van Daal, Jan (1996) 'From Utilitarianism to Hedonism: Gossen, Jevons and Walras', *The Journal of the History of Economic Thought* 18(2): 271–86.

Vasquez, Andrés (1997) 'The Awareness of Cournot's Recherches among Early British Economists', *Research in the History of Economic Thought and Methodology* 15: 115–37.

Wach, H. M. (1991) 'A "Still, Small Voice" from the Pulpit: Religion and the Creation of Social Morality in Manchester, 1820–1850', *Journal of Modern History* 63(3): 425–56.

—— (1993) 'Unitarian Philanthropy and Cultural Hegemony in Comparative Perspective: Manchester and Boston, 1827–1848', *Journal of Social History* 26(3): 539–57.

Wagner, A. (1864) *Die Gesetzmässigkeit in den scheinbar willkührlichen menschlichen Handlungen*. Hamburg: Boyes & Geisler.

Walker, F. A. (1891) 'The Doctrine of Rent, and the Residual Claimant Theory of Wages', *The Quarterly Journal of Economics* 5: 417–37.

Walras, L. [1874] (1988) *Eléments d'économie politique pure ou théorie de la richesse sociale*. Oeuvres Economiques Complètes Vol. VIII. Paris: Economica.

—— [1875] (1987) 'De l'application des mathématiques à l'économie politique', in: *Mélanges d'économie politique et sociale*. Oeuvres Économiques Complètes Vol. VII. Paris: Economica, 291–329.

Warke, T. (2000) 'Mathematical Fitness in the Evolution of the Utility Concept from Bentham to Jevons to Marshall', *Journal of the History of Economic Thought* 22(1): 5–27.

Waterman, A. M. C. (1991) *Revolution, Economics and Religion. Christian Political Economy, 1798–1833*. Cambridge: Cambridge University Press.

Webb, R. K. (1992) 'A Crisis of Authority: Early Nineteenth-Century British Thought', *Albion* 24(1): 1–16.

Wellens-De Donder L. (1966) *Inventaire de la correspondance d'Adolphe Quetelet*. Brussel: Palais des Académies.

Wells, S. (1997) 'William Ellery Channing Web Center' [http://www.geocities.com/Athens/5322/indexwecc.htm].

Westergaard, H. (1932) *Contributions to the History of Statistics*. London: King & Son.

Whitaker, J. K. (1984) 'Review of Papers and Correspondence of William Stanley Jevons, Volumes I–VII', *History of Political Economy* 16(1): 149–51.

White, M. V. (1982) 'Jevons in Australia: A Reassessment', *Economic Record* 58(160): 32–45.

—— (1984) 'Jevons in Australia: Response to Professor Hutchison', *The Manchester School* 52(1): 70–2.

—— (1989a) 'Jevons' Antipodean Interlude: Rejoinder', *History of Political Economy* 21(4): 623–31.

—— (1989b) 'Why Are There No Supply and Demand Curves in Jevons?', *History of Political Economy* 21(3): 425–56.

—— (1991a) 'A Biographical Puzzle: Why Did Jevons Write the Coal Question?', *Journal of the History of Economic Thought* 13: 222–42.

—— (1991b) 'Jevons' "Blunder" Concerning Value and Distribution: an Explanation', *Cambridge Journal of Economics* 15: 149–60.

—— (1991c) 'Jevons on Utility, Exchange, and Demand Theory: Comment', *The Manchester School* 59(1): 80–3.

—— (1991d) 'Where Did Jevons' Energy Come From?', *History of Economics Review* 15: 60–72.

—— (1991e) 'Frightening the "Landed Forgies": Parliamentary Politics and The Coal Question', *Utilitas* 3(2): 289–302.

—— (1993) 'The "Irish Factor" in Jevons' Statistics: a Note', *History of Economics Review* 19: 79–85.

—— (1994a) 'Jevons and the Population Mechanism: Comment', *The Manchester School* 62(1): 97–102.

—— (1994b) 'Bridging the Natural and the Social: Science and Character in Jevons' Political Economy', *Economic Inquiry* 32: 429–44.

—— (1994c) 'The Moment of Richard Jennings: the Production of Jevons' Marginalist Economic Agent', in: Mirowski, P. (ed.) *Natural Images in Economic Thought*. Cambridge: Cambridge University Press, 197–230.

—— (1994d) 'Following Strange Gods: Women in Jevons' Political Economy', in: Groenewegen, P. (ed.) *Feminism and Political Economy in Victorian England*. Aldershot: Edward Elgar, 46–78.

—— (1994e) 'A Five Per Cent Racist ? Rejoinder to Professor Hutchison', *History of Economics Review* 21: 71–86.

—— (1994f) ' "That God-Forgotten Thornton": Exorcising Higgling after On Labour', *History of Political Economy* 26(Suppl.): 149–83.

—— (1996) Notes on Jevons's 'On the Science of Art and Music' Manuscript, unpublished typescript.

—— (1999) 'Obscure Objects of Desire? Nineteenth-Century British Economists and the Price(s) of "Rare Art" ', in: De Marchi, N., and C. D. W. Goodwin (eds) Economic Engagements with Art. *History of Political Economy* Supplement: 57–84.

—— (2001) 'Indeterminacy in Exchange: Disinterring Jevons's Trading Bodies', *The Manchester School* 69(2): 208–26.

Wicksteed, P. H. [1885] (1988) 'The Jevonian Criticism of Marx: A Rejoinder', *Today: Monthly Magazine of Scientific Socialism*, New Series 3(4): 177–9, reprinted in: Wood, J. C. (ed.) *William Stanley Jevons: Critical Assessments*, Vol. II. London: Routledge, 106–8.

—— [1889] (1988) 'On Certain Passages in Jevons' Theory of Political Economy', *Quarterly Journal of Economics* 3: 293–314, reprinted in: Wood, J. C. (ed.) *William Stanley Jevons: Critical Assessments*, Vol. II. London: Routledge, 28–45.

—— [1905] (1988) 'Jevons' Economic Work', *Economic Journal* 15: 432–6, reprinted in: Wood, J. C. (ed.) *William Stanley Jevons: Critical Assessments*, Vol. III. London: Routledge, 11–14.

Wilbur, E. M. (1946) *A History of Unitarianism: Socinianism and its Antecedents*. Cambridge, MA: Harvard University Press.

Williamson, Oliver E. (1981) 'The Economics of Organization: The Transaction Cost Approach', *American Journal of Sociology* 87: 548–77.

Winch, D. (1972) 'Marginalism and the Boundaries of Economic Science', *History of Political Economy* 4(2): 325–43.

Wood, J. C. (ed.) (1988a) *William Stanley Jevons: Critical Assessments*, three volumes. London: Routledge.

—— (1988b) 'General Commentary', in: Wood, J. C. (ed.) *William Stanley Jevons: Critical Assessments*, Vol. I. London: Routledge, 3–8.

—— (1988c) 'Commentary', in: Wood, J. C. (ed.) *William Stanley Jevons: Critical Assessments*, Vol. II. London: Routledge, 3–4.

—— (1988d) 'Commentary', in: Wood, J. C. (ed.) *William Stanley Jevons: Critical Assessments*, Vol. II. London: Routledge, 87–8.

—— (1988e) 'Commentary', in: Wood, J. C. (ed.) *William Stanley Jevons: Critical Assessments*, Vol. III. London: Routledge, 3–8.

Young, A. A. [1912] (1988) 'Jevons' Theory of Political Economy', *American Economic Review* 2(1): 576–89, reprinted in: Wood, J. C. (ed.) *William Stanley Jevons: Critical Assessments*, Vol. II. London: Routledge, 51–62.

Zouboulakis, M. (1997) 'Mill and Jevons: Two Concepts of Economic Rationality', *History of Economic Ideas* 5(2): 7–25.

Index

For Product Safety Concerns and Information please contact our EU
representative GPSR@taylorandfrancis.com Taylor & Francis Verlag GmbH,
Kaufingerstraße 24, 80331 München, Germany

Printed and bound by CPI Group (UK) Ltd, Croydon, CR0 4YY
08/05/2025
01864412-0010